RUDIMENTS

OF THE

HEBREW GRAMMAR.

RUDIMENTS

OF THE

HEBREW GRAMMAR

TRANSLATED

FROM THE SEVENTH LATIN EDITION OF

VOSEN-KAULEN'S „RUDIMENTA"

BY

H. GABRIELS,

RECTOR OF ST JOSEPH'S SEMINARY, TROY, N Y.

WIPF & STOCK · Eugene, Oregon

Wipf and Stock Publishers
199 W 8th Ave, Suite 3
Eugene, OR 97401

Rudiments of the Hebrew Grammar
Translated from the Seventh Latin Edition of
Vosen-Kaulen's "Rudimenta"
By Gabriels, H. and Vosen, C. H.
Softcover ISBN-13: 978-1-6667-4078-3
Hardcover ISBN-13: 978-1-6667-4079-0
eBook ISBN-13: 978-1-6667-4080-6
Publication date 2/18/2022
Previously published by B. Herder, 1888

This edition is a scanned facsimile of
the original edition published in 1888.

PREFACE.

There is no lack of grammars of the Hebrew language written in English, but none of them have as yet been found so complete, while yet so brief, as Vosen-Kaulen's 'Rudimenta', of which we here present a translation By its successive editions, both in Latin and in German, this justly esteemed manual has proved that it fills a want, which makes itself every day more strongly felt in ecclesiastical schools. While necessarily short, it gives in a methodical and precise manner all the ordinary grammatical forms of the language and the principal rules of its syntax Experience has shown that by means of this unpretending little volume a knowledge of Hebrew can be acquired that will be found sufficient for the greater number of theological students The 'Rudimenta' indeed fully answer the requirements of the one year's course of Hebrew, prescribed by the Third Plenary Council of Baltimore, while for scholars, desirous of ampler knowledge, they prove a useful and solid introduction to more exhaustive grammars

For this purpose, however, the German edition is available for a few pupils only, and the Latin text, on account of its intricacies and obscurities, makes the study of Hebrew unnecessarily laborious and even repulsive We have, therefore, with the cooperation of the proprietor, Mr. Herder, and under the supervision of Vosen's editor, undertaken to publish the 'Rudimenta' in English, and so the old work in its new garb is hereby offered to the young scholars of the sanctuary, with a fond hope that it will aid them in their study of the holy Scriptures of the Old Testament, which can also instruct unto salvation, through the faith which is in Christ Jesus. (II Tim III, 15)

Troy N Y, feast of S Joseph, 1888.

H. Gabriels.

CONTENTS.

Contents

Introduction.

A sketch of the Hebrew language.

The Hebrew language is a member of the Semitic family of languages, among which it approaches the nearest to the Phenician and the Punic, although also closely related to the Arabic, the Assyrian and the Aramaïc Hebrew was the language of those descendants of Sem, who, after the dispersion of the sons of Noe settled in Palestine and lived there long after under various names, as v g Zuzim, Kadmonim, etc. In the course of time the Canaanites immigrated into Palestine and adopted the language of the country, which on this account received the name of *leshôn cená'an*, "the tongue of Canaan" It was from the Canaanites that Abraham, whose native tongue was Aramaïc learned it, and by him it was transmitted to his descendants, the Israelites These the Canaanites called ʿ*Ibhrîm*, Ἑβραῖοι and as this name was more commonly in use among the surrounding nations than that of Israelites, their language itself was afterwards called Hebrew Hebrew, however, after the Babylonian captivity gradually passed out of use and became a dead language, as it was supplanted by the Aramaïc or Syro-Chaldaic. Afterwards the Rabbis and the writers of the Talmud formed from the old Hebrew a new language which is called New-Hebrew (Talmudic and Rabbinic).

Hebrew was used as a Literary language while the Jews remained an independent people; but no documents written in it have come down to us, except the Holy Scriptures and some inscriptions and coins

Writing in Hebrew was from the beginning alphabetic, and was founded originally on an alphabet which was common to all Semitic peoples, having been formed from the hieratic writing of the Egyptians. This alphabet is commonly called the Phenician alphabet, and has ever after been preserved by the Samaritans to write not only the Samaritan but even the Hebrew The Jews on the contrary during the captivity began to use in its stead the Assyrian or Square Alphabet which, however, is only a calligraphic modification of the ancient characters. The square alphabet has ever since been used to write Hebrew, except on coins.

Note In regard to the pronunciation of Hebrew, there are no traditional rules that are certain The modern Jews themselves do not agree on the subject, the German and Russian Hebrews pronouncing the language quite differently from those of Spain and Portugal It is the pronunciation of the latter that is generally followed by christian scholars

Book I.
Orthography.

⨯ § 1. The way of writing Hebrew.

For some centuries after the dispersion of the Jews, Hebrew was written with consonants only, and it was not until the language ceased completely to be spoken that for the preservation of the traditional reading of the holy text the necessity of vowel-signs was imperiously felt This want was supplied by the vowel-points, invented by the doctors of Tiberias. Henceforth the text remained indeed as before, consisting of the old consonant signs only; but points, indicating the vowel sound as known by tradition, were written over or under or even in the consonant

Hebrew is written from right to left, and Hebrew books, both manuscript and printed, have ordinarily their beginning where ours end, that is to say, their first page is at the right and the last at the left side of the volume.

⨯ § 2. The Alphabet.

Hebrew has twenty-two consonant letters. One of them, however, the twenty-first, may stand for *s* or for *sh*, according to the place in which it is marked by its *diacritical dot*, so that the twenty-two characters represent twenty-three sounds.

These same letters serve also to express the numerals, according to a very ancient rule which is common to all Semitic languages, as shown in the following table.

Hebrew Letters have the following

form	name	pronunciation	numerical value
א	'Aleph	⸗ (slight aspiration)	1
ב	Bêth	b, bh, v	2
ג	Gímel	g, gh	3
ד	Daleth	d, dh	4
ה	He	h	5
ו	Vav	v, w	6
ז	Zayın	z	7
ח	Chêth	ch, kh (strong aspiration)	8
ט	Têth	t	9
י	Jôdh	y (German j)	10
כ, final ך	Caph	c (as in cap), ch	20
ל	Lamedh	l	30
מ, final ם	Mêm	m	40
נ, final ן	Nûn	n	50
ס	Samech	s	60
ע	'Ayin	⸗ (strong guttural)	70
פ, final ף	Pê	p, ph	80
צ, final ץ	Tsadhê	ts	90
ק	Kôph	k, q	100
ר	Rêsch	r	200
שׂ	Sîn	s	} 300
שׁ	Shîn	sh	
ת	Tav	t, th	400

Note   The letter 'Aleph is pronounced very lightly like the Spiritus lenis of the Greek. Zaın ın the Septuagint and Vulgate is always represented by Z, v g זברי Ζαβδί, זוזים Zuzim 'Ayın had a guttural and very hard sound, the true pronunciation of which cannot easily be described   The Galıleans at the tıme of Christ pronounced ıt like 'Aleph, and hence ıt is now generally neglected

in reading at least when it begins a syllable; at the end many pronounce it something like *ng* in *hang* The Greek version and the Vulgate render it often by H or G, v g עברי ʽEβραῖος, עמרה *Gomorrha.*
Tsadê in the same translations is everywhere S, v g צמרים *Samaraim*

§ 3. The writing of the letters.

The letters *Caph*, *Mêm*, *Nûn*, *Pê*, *Tsadhê* at the end
of words are written in an other form than in the middle,
viz. ך ם ן ף ץ. These forms are called final letters, and
compose the mnemonic word כמנפץ *(camnéphets).*

Words are not divided at the end of a line; hence if
the line should otherwise not be full, the letters *'Aleph*,
He, *Lamedh*, *final Mêm* and *Tav* are extended thus: א,
ה, ל, ם, ת, and are therefore called distensible letters.
They compose the mnemonic word: אֲהַלְתָּם *(ᵃhaltem).*

When used as numerals, the Hebrew letters from א
to ט stand for monads, for decads from י to צ, and for
the hundreds from ק to ת. The character ש without either
dot counts for 300 After ת which stands for 400, the
hundreds are expressed by the five final letters. From
one thousand up, the same letters used to express the
monads etc. are employed, but the difference in the value
is indicated by two dots written over them, as בּ = 2000.
To combine the monads, the decads and the hundreds, the
letters are placed in juxta-position, reading the greater values
first from right to left, v. g תלו = 436 Fifteen is the only
exception, being expressed by טו 9 + 6, not יה 10 + 5,
because these two letters stand for the holy name of God.

§ 4. Vowel-letters and vowel-points.

All the vowels of human speech can be reduced to
three principal sounds, viz. of *a* (as in *father*), *i* (as in
sister), *u* (as in *rude*). Other sounds are either a middle
between them, as *e* (in *let*) between *a* and *i*, *o* between *a*
and *u*, *u* (sounded as in French) between *u* and *i*, or else

they combine into diphthongs as the English *ou* and *ei*.
The Hebrew language, however, has no diphthongs, and only
possesses the two medium sounds *e* and *o*; hence there are
in Hebrew five vowels *a, e, ı, o, u*, which being both long
and short, make ten vowel-sounds altogether.

Vowel-letters. The long vowels are often expressed
in the Bible by the consonants 'Aleph, Jôdh, Vav and also
at the end of words by He; א standing for *a*, י for *i*,
ו for *u*, and the middlesounds being rendered, *e* by א, י
and ה, *o* by א, ו and ה; v. g קאם *kâm*, שׂים *sîm*, לון *lûn*,
צאת *tsêth*, בין *bén*, צאן *tsôn*, יום *yôm*, היה *hayâ*. Hence
these four consonants are called vowel-letters, semi-vowels
or *matres lectionis* (mothers of the reading). A long vowel
thus expressed is said to be written **fully**, otherwise
defectively, as גר *gar*, מת *meth*, אם *'ım*, כל *kol*, קם *kum*.

Vowel-points. Besides the vowel-letters, other
signs were invented, as was noted before, to indicate all
the vowels by being affixed to the consonants. Of such
characters there are nine, and as one of them serves to
indicate both the long and the short sound of the same
vowel it may in a wide sense be said that there are five
long and five short vowel-points, as follows:

Form	Name	Pronunciation
ָ	קָמֵץ *Kámets*	ā
ֵ	צרי *Tserê*	ē
־ִי	חִירָק גָּדוֹל *Chîrek gadhôl*	ī
ֹ , ו	חוֹלֶם *Chôlem*	ō
ו	שׁוּרָק *Shûrek*	ū
ַ	פַּתַח *Pathach*	ă
ֶ	סגול *Seghôl*	ĕ
ִ	חִירָק קָטוֹן *Chîrek katon*	ĭ
ָ	קָמֶץ חָטוּף *Kâmets chatúph*	ŏ
ֻ	קִבּוּץ *Kibbúts*	ŭ (sometimes long)

These signs are affixed to the consonants as they are here to the dashes, over or under them, Shûrek being always written in the bosom of the Vav In reading, the consonant is pronounced first, the vowel after, as סָ *sa*, סֶ *se*, ס *so*, etc To this rule there is one exception, viz. of the *Pathach furtivum*, which is pronounced before its consonant, as explained below, § 11 n. 3.

Quiescent vowel-letters When the Masoretes or punctuators added the vowel-points to the old consonants, they did not omit the vowel-letters from the text, so that now the same vowel is indicated by the two kinds of signs, v g רֹאשׁ *râsh*, קִיר *kîr*, צֵא *tsé*, אֵין *'én*, רֹאשׁ *rôsh*, קוֹל *kôl*. In such a case the vowel-letter or *mater lectionis* is said to be *quiescent* or *silent*. The Vav alone is never quiescent in Kibbûts, but always in Shûrek

At the end of words *He* frequently quiesces in *a, e,* or *o,* v g. הָיָה *hayâ*, חֹזֶה *chozê*, רָאֹה *ra'ô*; when not quiescent, it is noted by a dot, called מַפִּיק *mappîk*, v. g אַרְצָה *'artsah*.

Note 1 Seghôl sometimes is used for a long vowel so that א, ה and י become quiescent in it, v g מִצֵּאן *metsêna* (v. § 42) רֵעָה *ro'ê*, שְׁתִינָה *shethênâ*

2. Cholem always coalesces with the diacritical point of שׁ, v. g שֹׂנֵא *sonê*, מֹשֶׁה *Moshê*, עֹשֶׂה *'osê*, שֹׁמֵר *shomer* The sign וֹ is ô, when no other vowel precedes or follows, v g לָשׁוֹן *lashon*; it is *vo*, when another vowel precedes, v g עָוֹן *'avon*; but it is *ov*, when another vowel is written under it, v g. לֹוֶה *lovê*

3. The Kamets-chatûph There is but one sign for the Kamets and the Kamets-chatûph To distinguish between the two becomes easy by practice only Meanwhile beginners may take for the theoretical general rule that the sign ָ is the short *o*, whenever it occurs in a *closed* (§ 14) syllable which has not the *accent* (§ 9) v g. חָכְמָה *chŏchmâ*, וַיָּקָם *vayyákŏm* Secondly, in a syllable that ends in a vowel the sound of ָ is *ŏ*, whenever it is followed by another short *o*, v g. תָּעָבְדֵם *to'ŏbhdem*, בָּחֳרִי *bochŏrî* (§ 18) Thirdly ָ is *ŏ* in קָדָשִׁים *kŏdhashîm*, and שֳׁרָשִׁים *shŏrashîm*.

4. The Cethîbh and the Kerî In the text of the Bible, vowels

are frequently affixed to a word or even to a supposed word, which
vocalize not any word of the text, but a word which is written in
the margin or at the foot of the page, and which is indicated in
the text by the sign ֯ or ֗ This signifies that the word of the
text was considered by the Masoretes as a wrong reading, and that
according to them it should be replaced or supplemented by the
word which they wrote in the margin or below. The reading of the
text, the wrong one, they called Cᵉthîbh *(written)* and the right one,
Kᵉrî *(read)*. The right reading is noted in several Rabbinical ex-
pressions, as קרי ולא כתיב *read but not written*, etc which must
be learned practically Some corrections that would have to be
repeated frequently are made by vowel-points belonging to the
right reading without any *Cᵉthîbh*, v. g הוא for היא; they are called
Kᵉrî perpetuum

§ 5. The Shᵉvâ.

Even vowelless consonants were marked with a sign
by the punctuators This was done by means of the שְׁוָא
Shᵉvâ or *vacuity*, thus called, because it indicates that the
consonant is void of a vowel. It has the form of our colon
— and is written under the consonants, as יְ, מְ, קְ. The
last letters of a word, although vowelless, do not take the
Shᵉvâ, as אָב *'âbh*, הֵן *hen*; except the letter Caph, as אֵיךְ
'êch, לָךְ *lach*, and except also a consonant that follows
another Shᵉvâ, as קָשְׁט *kasht*, אַתְּ = אַתְתְ (§ 8, 2)

Consonants that have a Shᵉvâ are either at the beginning or at the end of a syllable In the first case the
Shᵉvâ is pronounced like a very short *e*, and is called
movable or rather vocal; in the latter it is not pronounced and is called silent. Thus in the word קְטַלְתֶּם, the
first Shᵉvâ is vocal, the second silent, and the word reads
kᵉtaltem.

The Shᵉvâ thus far described, both vocal and silent,
is called the *simple Shᵉvâ*, and is not to be confounded
with the *compound Shᵉvâ* or *Chateph* of the next paragraph.

Note   To know when a Sheᵊvâ is vocal observe the following
rules   It begins the syllable and is consequently vocal, a) under
the first letter of any word; b) after a long vowel; c) under a double
consonant *(having a Daghesh forte);* d) when it follows another Sheᵊvâ

§ 6. The Compound Sheᵊvâ or Chateph.

The vocal Sheᵊvâ stands sometimes not for a very short
sound of *e,* but for the shortest possible sound of the three
short vowels *a, e* and *o.* To show this, the sign of those
vowels is written to the left of the two dots, thus —֙ —֔ —֗.
This Sheᵊvâ is called the *compound Sheᵊvâ* or חָטֵף *Chateph.*
It is threefold:

a) Chateph-pathach, as in the word חֲלֹא *hᵃlô.*

b) Chateph-seghôl, as in אֱכֹל *ᵉchol.*

c) Chateph-kamets, standing for a very short *o* חֳלִי *chᵒlî.*

× § 7. Doubling of letters by the Daghesh-forte.

When a consonant should be doubled, it is written
only once, with a dot in the bosom of the letter   This
doubling point is called דָּגֵשׁ כָּבֵד Daghesh-forte, v g
קַטָּל *kuttal.*

Note 1   The *Daghesh-forte* is not written in the final letters of
words, v. g. עַז *ᶜazz,* דַּל *dall,* עַם *ᶜamm*

2.   Likewise the *Daghesh-forte* is omitted in letters that have a
Sheᵊvâ, and this always in י, mostly in ל, מ, נ; sometimes iu ק and
ט, and sometimes also in the other consonants, v g וַיְהִי *vayyᵉhi,*
הַלְלוּ *hallᵉlû,* הִנְנִי *hinnᵉnî,* הַמְבַקְשִׁים *hammᵉbhakkᵉshîm.*

3.   Vav with the Daghesh-forte has the same form as the Shûrek
וּ; to know which it is, see whether a vowel precedes and follows
it.   If so, it is a Daghesh-forte עִוּר *ᶜivver;* if between consonants,
it is Shûrek, עוּר *ᶜûr*

× § 8. Removing the aspiration by the Daghesh-lene;
the Raphe.

Six consonants Bêth, Gîmel, Daleth, Caph, Pê and Tav
lose their native aspiration when they follow a consonant,

*

but retain it when they follow a vowel or a vocal Shᵉvâ.
This loss of the aspiration is indicated by a dot like the
Daghesh-forte, but which is called *Daghesh-lene*, v. g. קָרְב
kerebh becomes קִרְבּוֹ *kirbô*, because here the Bêth follows
a consonant; thus also זָגַר *zaghar* becomes לִזְגֹר *lizgor*, etc
These six letters are comprised in the mnemonic בְּגַד־כְּפַת
bᵉghadh-cᵉphath

The Daghesh-lene is consequently written: a) in the
beginning of any sentence (of a book, of a phrase, of a
division of a phrase), b) in the beginning of a word, when
the preceding word ends in a consonant, v g. עַל כֵּן, c) in
the middle and at the end of words, where a simple Shᵉvâ
precedes, v. g. קְטַלְתֶּם *kᵉtaltem*, קְטַלְתְּ *kᵉtalt*, d) and finally
even after a word ending in a vowel, when this vowel has
a disjunctive accent, since then the aspirate is regarded as
removed from the influence of the vowel, as בְּצַלְמֵנוּ כִּדְמוּתֵנוּ
in our image, like our likeness.

Note 1   The Raphe   Formerly when these six letters remained
aspirates, they where marked with a dash over the letter that was
called a רָפֶה *Raphe*   The same was done for the letter He, when
it was not marked with a Mappîk   Afterwards this sign was ordinarily omitted, and is but seldom retained in the editions of the
Bible, v. g   Zach IV, 7 הָרֹאשָׁה *harôshâ*

2   The Daghesh-forte in these letters doubles their inaspirate
sound, v g   עַכּוֹ *'accô*, נֻפַּח *nuppach*.

3   The Daghesh in the six aspirates is known as forte if it
immediately follows a vowel; otherwise it is lene, v. g   לִסְבֹּךְ *lisboch*,
סִבֵּךְ *sibbech*

4   An aspirate that follows a consonant with a Shᵉvâ at the
end of an apocopated word (§§ 43, 90) keeps its Daghesh-lene, v g
וַיֵּשֶׁב apocopated from וַיֵּשְׁבָּה, וַיֵּבְךְּ from וַיִּבְכֶּה.

5.   שָׁלַחַת (§ 35) is written for שָׁלַחְתְּ (§ 18. 1, note 2) keeping
its Daghesh-lene and its Shᵉvâ (§ 5)

§ 9. The accent.

Hebrew words as a general rule have the accent on
the last syllable; a few have it on the penult; none on

the antepenult. Thus the words are either מִלְרַע *milra‘*, that is ὀξύτονα, v. g מָלַךְ *malách*, or מלעיל *mil‘él*, that is παροξύτονα, v. g מֹלֶךְ *mélech*.

The punctuators marked each word with an accent, and this in such a manner as to indicate thereby the relative force of every word in the sentence. Thus these accent-signs assist not only the pronunciation, but also the interpretation of the text, and fill the office of our punctuation signs

For this purpose the accents are divided into two classes: those which indicate that a word must be separated from the following, and are called disjunctive, and those that join one word with the next, and are therefore called conjunctive accents

Both classes are written either over or under the words, v g סֹפר *sépher*, כתֹב *c^ethóbh*; either at the beginning or at the end, v. g תָּאבד *tobhédh*, קָטַל *katál*, דָּבָ֫ר *débher*; nearly all (the prepositive accents ⌐, — and ⌐, and the postpositive ⌐, ˊ, ˆ, ˋ and ⌐ excepted) are placed on the syllable which has the tonic accent, v g הֻגַּד *huggádh*, יֵשֶׁבֶת *yoshébheth*

Of the thirty-two Hebrew accents we give here only the principal disjunctive or distinctive ones which are equivalent to our full stop, colon and semicolon

— *Sillûk* which is always placed under the last word, (and in biblical sentences always followed by the Sôph-pasûk ׃—); thus equivalent to our full stop.

— *'Athnach* which separates the two principal members of the sentence as our colon or semicolon.

⌐ *S^eghóltâ* which is placed on the last word of parts of a sentence and has as substitute the *Shalsheleth* —.

— *Zakeph katon* subdivides the principal members of the phrase as does its substitute, the *Zakeph gadhól* —.

— *Tiphchâ*, slight subdivision.

॒ *Rᵉbíá* announces frequently the direct speech of another.

॒ *Mêrᵉcha mahpachatum*, the same as the 'Athnach, used in poetical verses.

Note 1   The Jews divide the accents into kings, dukes, counts and servants

2. Words with more than two syllables, if ὀξύτονοι receive a sign called *Methegh* ॒, which usually falls upon the second syllable before the accent and represents a minor stress of the voice. In this case a simple or compound vocal Shᵉvâ counts as a syllable, v. g. עֲהָדִי *sàhᵃdhî*, כְּבְדוּ *càbᵉdhû*, and therefore Ps CXLIV, 14 מְסֻבָּלִים, Ruth I, 11 בְּמֵעַי

3. Hence the *Methegh* serves often to show, whether a syllable is closed or open, and thus whether ॒ is Kamets or Kamets-chatûph, v. g. קָטְלוּ *kŏt-lû*, קָטְלוּ *ka-tᵉ-lû* Without Methegh the sign ॒ before a letter with simple Shᵉvâ is always Kamets-chatûph; with it, it is commonly Kamets

4. Some words have two accents, a principal and a secondary one. The latter may be placed on syllables before the penult, v. g. תְּשׁוּקָתֵךְ.

Book II.
Grammar.

Chapter I.
The elements of speech.

§ 10. Various kinds of letters.

The consonants are divided into different classes on account of the organ with which, or of the manner in which they are enunciated

First they are:

gutturals א, ה, ח, ע (אַהַחַע),

palatals ג, י, כ, ק (גִיכַק),

linguals ד, ת, ט, ל, נ (דַטלנת),

dentals ז, ס, צ, שׁ (זַסצַשׁ),

labials פ, מ, ו, ב (בוּמַף)

The ר holds a kind of middle place between the gutturals and the linguals and follows nearly always the rules of the gutturals

Secondly they are:

mutes ב, ג, ד, ה, ח, ט, כ, ע, פ, ק, ת,

liquids ל, מ, נ, ר,

sibilants ס, שׁ, שׂ, ז, צ,

semivowels א, ו, י, ה

§ 11. Properties of the gutturals.

1 The gutturals א, ה, ח, ע are always accompanied by a compound instead of a vocal Sheᵛâ   א has a preference for the Chateph-seghôl, the others for Chateph-pathach,

עֲדִי, חֲמָשִׁים, חֲלֹא, אֲבָל g. ‪v.‬ The gutturals sometimes admit the silent Sh°vâ, v. g. הֶעָדִיף, אֶחְדַל, יֶהֱגֶה, נֶאְדָּר, sometimes reject it as in הָעֳמַד, מֳעֳמָד, יַעֲמִיד, in which latter case they take the Chateph which agrees with the preceding vowel.

2 The Daghesh-forte is never written in the gutturals, though two of them, which can be doubled in the pronunciation, the ה and the ח, may on that account receive an implicit Daghesh-forte Hence when according to grammatical rules the guttural should be doubled, the א and the ע, to compensate for the Daghesh, lengthen the preceding vowel, but ה and ח receive the implicit Daghesh-forte and the preceding vowel is consequently not lengthened, v. g. הָאָדָם for הַאָדָם, צָעַק for צִעֵק, but מַהֵר for מַהֵר and נִחַם for נֶחַם.

Note. The letter ר follows the peculiarity of א and ע, v g. בְּרָךְ for בֵּרַךְ, הָרֹאשׁ for הָרֹאשׁ It is, however, also found doubled, as in Prov. XIV, 10 מָרַת *moirath*

3. The gutturals have a general preference for the sound of *a*. Hence, where according to the rules of inflection, other vowels would be required, they take *a*, except א which prefers the Chateph-seghôl, v g. the regular form of the future being *o*, יִשְׁלֹף *yishloph*, with a guttural it is *a*, יִשְׁלַח *yishlach*.

4. The Pathach-furtive. On account of this nature of the gutturals, when, at the end of words, any long vowel, different from *a*, precedes ה, ח or ע, a very short *a* is inserted under, and pronounced before the guttural, this being the only case, as mentioned at § 4, where a vowel is pronounced before the consonant under which it is written, v. g. גְּבֹהַּ *gabhóah*, רוּחַ *rúach*, הִשְׁמִיעַ *hishmía*, יָרֵחַ *yaréach*, יְהוֹשֻׁעַ *y°hóschúa* This Pathach, stealing in, as it were, between two such letters, is called פַּתַח גְּנוּבָה Pathach-furtive. Before the א or the ה it is not required, because these letters, more than the others, partake of the nature of vowels.

§ 12. Semivowels.

1. א, י, ו (and also ה at the end of words) are so akin to vowels that they sometimes divest themselves of their peculiar nature and become vowels; hence they are used instead of vowels and thus become quiescent (§ 4). Those vowel sounds that agree with each quiescent letter, as *a*, *e*, *o* with 'Aleph, *e*, *ı* with Yôdh, *o*, *u* with Vav are called its *homogenous* vowels, the others being *heterogenous* to the semivowel with which they do not agree.

2. It is to be noted that the first three semivowels א, י, ו always become vowels and are quiescent whenever at the end of a syllable they receive a homogenous vowel, v. g. לָאמֹר for לאמֹר (that is לָא־מֹר), בִּיהוּדָה for בִיהוּדָה, צֵאת for צְאת הוּשַׁב for הוּשׁב. *He* follows the same rule at the end of a word, v. g. יֵהְיֶה, גָּלָה, אָשָׂה   More about this will be said hereafter.

Note   The semivowels quiesce mostly in long vowels; but we find also לַאדְנָי for לַאדֹנָי

§ 13. Assimilation of consonants.

1. A consonant with a silent Sh⁽e⁾vâ, preceding a like consonant, combines with the latter into a double letter which is written only once, but with a Daghesh-forte, v. g. הִתַּמֵּר for הִתְתַמֵּר, שַׁתָּה for שַׁתְתָה.

2. *Nûn* in a similar position assimilates itself with any following consonant, v g אַתֶּם for אַנְתֶּם, מְקֶדֶם for מִנְקֶדֶם, מִזֶּה for מִנְזֶה. Sometimes ל, ת and ה are likewise assimilated, v g יִקַּח for יִלְקַח, הִנַּבֵּא for הִתְנַבֵּא, מַחְזֶה for מַהְזֶה.

Note. Very often *He* is assimilated not with the following, but with the preceding *Nûn*, v. g יִקְטְלֶנּוּ for יִקְטְלֶנְהוּ.

As in Hebrew no syllables begin with a vowel, the syllables are distinguished by their termination, and this into three classes:

1. O p e n or s i m p l e syllables, which end in a vowel, v. g לוֹ.

2. C l o s e d or m i x e d syllables, which end in a consonant, v. g. בַּיִת.

3. A c u t e or s h a r p syllables, that end in a consonant combined with another by a Daghesh-forte

Note. There are also i n t e r m e d i a t e syllables in which a consonant, not doubled, completes the syllable that precedes and begins the one that follows, v. g חָהֲרגוּ *ta‿ha‿re ghû̂ ta‿ha‿* are both intermediate syllables. Consonants in this equivocal relation are such as remain single when they should have been doubled, or are sounded when they might have had a silent Shevâ, or are preceded by a vowel which has arisen from a Shevâ

A consonant, with a simple or compound vocal Shevâ, does not form a syllable, but is considered as an increment of the next syllable; v g in יִתקַטְּלוּ *yithkatt^elû*, there are three syllables, the first of which *yith* is closed, the second *kat* sharp, the third *t^elû*, open   (See however, § 9, note 2.)

Note   There is one syllable in Hebrew apparently commencing with a vowel, viz ו from the conjunction ו when it begins some words, v. g וּמִי.

§ 15. Vowels of the different syllables.

O p e n syllables have l o n g vowels, when they are unaccented. If accented, whether open or closed, syllables may indifferently contain a long or a short vowel.

C l o s e d syllables, unaccented, have s h o r t vowels.

S h a r p syllables have s h o r t vowels

Note 1. See § 4, note 3 about the discrimination of the Kamets-chatûph

2. A few words have sharp syllables, if accented, long, v g. אַכָּה and some forms of the verbs עע, see § 39, form Hiphil.

⨯ § 16. Union of words. The Makkeph.

Sometimes two or more words are so intimately united that when spoken they seem to be only one word. This is noted:

a) By the Daghesh-forte c o n j u n c t i v u m, which is marked in the first letter of the latter word, almost only after the quiescent ה, v. g נָתַתָּה לִּי *nathattâllî, thou hast given me*, אַרְצָה גֹּשֶׁן *'artsâggóshĕn, into the land of Goshen.*

b) By the copulative sign or hyphen which is called Makkeph, v. g וַיְהִי־כֵן *vayehîchen, and it was so*, כִּי־טוב *kîtôb, that (it was) good.*

c) By the Daghesh and the Makkeph together, v. g. בּוֹנֶה־בַּיִת *bônebbáyith, building a house*, גְּשָׁה־נָא *geshânnâ, approach, pray*

All the words joined in such a manner are considered as one word only and have only one accent. The first word or words have therefore their vowels shortened, and they are not seldom fused into one word, as מִזֶּה for מְה זֶּה, מַה־לָּכֶם, מֶה לָּכֶם for מַה־לָּכֶם, and these were for מַה־זֶּה, מֶה־זֶּה

N o t e   As the vowel is shortened in the syllable preceding the Makkeph, it follows that the sign ָ before it is a Kamets-chatûph, v. g כָּל־אִשָּׁה *every woman.*

§ 17. Changes of vowels.

1 When by declension or otherwise, vowels from open or accented become closed or unaccented, and viceversa, they change consequently their quantity. Hence l o n g vowels become s h o r t:

a) When the accent is removed from a final closed syllable, v. g יָקָם becomes וַיָּקָם, יֵשֵׁב – וַיֵּשֶׁב, אוֹב – אֹבְךָ, חִקִּי – חק, אִמִּי – אם, יִקְטְלֵם – יִקְטֹל

b) When an open syllable becomes closed, v. g ספר *book*, ספרי *my book*, קֹדֶשׁ *sanctuary*, קָדְשִׁי *my sanctuary*

N o t e   Tserê is generally shortened into the small Chîrek, sometimes into Seghôl; the Chôlem generally becomes Kamets-chatûph, but also Kibbûts when followed by a Daghesh-forte

2 S h o r t vowels are transmuted into l o n g ones:

a) When a closed syllable becomes open, v. g מָוֶת–מוּת, הָרִים – הַר, ספּר – ספר

b) When the syllable should be acute, but cannot
v. g on account of a guttural (§ 11, 2), as בָּרַךְ for בְּרַךְ,
שָׁעַר for שָׁעַר.

c) When a semivowel accedes and quiesces in a vowel;
see § 12, 2, v. g. לֵאמֹר for לֵאמֹר.

d) On account of the emphasis of disjunctive accents
in a pause, as בַּדֶּרֶךְ for בַּדֶּרֶךְ (see § 20).

Note 1   Observe that Chîrek parvum becomes always Tserê,
and that Kibbûts transmutes into Chôlem.

2. These rules are mechanical explanations for the sake of
beginners, not true grammatical deductions.

⌐ § 18. Formation of new vowels and syllables.

1. It is but seldom that two consonants end a word
without a vowel between them; generally in such a case
a vowel is inserted, v. g נַעַר for נַעַר, יִגֶל for יִגְל, זַיִת
for זַיִת.

Note 1   The additional vowel is ordinarily Seghôl; a guttural
takes Pathach; a quiescible letter requires a homogenous vowel.
See examples just given

2   To this rule the 2. person singular fem. (§ 24) of Perfect
in verbs is an exception, v g. קָטַלְתְּ, נִקְטַלְתְּ; yet in this case gutturals
require a Pathach, v. g. שָׁלַחַתְּ for שָׁלַחַתְּ. Particular exceptions are
forms like נֵרְדְּ, קְשֹׁטְ, וַיַּשְׁבְּ

2. It is likewise forbidden to begin a word with three
consonants. To avoid this, three remedies are used:

a) A vocal Sheˆvâ before another simple Sheˆvâ is changed
into Chîrek, v g. לִקְטֹל for לְקְטֹל, כִּנְפֹּל for כְּנְפֹּל.

b) A vocal Sheˆvâ before a compound Sheˆvâ changes
into the vowel which agrees with the Chateph, v. g. לַעֲמֹד
for לְעֲמֹד, בַּחֲלִי for בְּחֲלִי

c) A compound Sheˆvâ before a simple Sheˆvâ changes
into the vowel which agrees with the Chateph itself, v g.
פָּעֳלָה for פָּעֳלָה, נֶאֶכְלוּ for נֶאֶכְלוּ, יַעֲמְדוּ for יַעֲמְדוּ.

3. Very frequently the simple Sheˆvâ which precedes
a syllable with the accent is changed into Kamets. Of

this we give as examples לָמַס for לְמַס, לָבֶטַח for לְבְטַח,
טוֹב וְרַע for טוֹב וְרַע, קָטֵל for קְטֵל. This important grammatical law may be noticed especially in declensions and
conjugations in which it causes many changes.

4. Besides, new vowels or syllables arise when the
accent lays more stress on some consonants, as is explained
in § 20

§ 19. Elision of vowels.

When trough a grammatical change, an increment,
beginning with a vowel, is added to a word, the accent
goes forward to this vowel, and the vowel which before
was the last, unless it was written *fully* (§ 4), is thrown
out or elided Thus from קְטֹל comes קָטְלוּ, from סֵפֶר—סְפָרִים;
but גְבוֹר makes גְבוּרִים Kamets in the syllable before the
accent (§ 18, 3) is elided whenever the accent is thrown
forward, v. g from קָטַל we have קָטַלְתִּי and קְטַלְתֶּם, קְטָלַנִי.

§ 20. Pauses.

The greater stress which is laid on the endings of
sentences or clauses of sentences, marked with distinctive
accents, is called a pause, and produces various effects, of
which the following are the most notable.

a) A short syllable, which receives the accent, becomes
long in a pause Thus קָטֵל becomes קָטֵל; מַיִם becomes
אֶרֶץ – אָרֶץ, מָיִם

b) When the last syllable has the accent and is preceded by a vocal Shevâ, this Shevâ in a pause is changed
into a long vowel which receives the accent, v. g. קְטֹלוּ
in a pause becomes קָטֹלוּ, מְלֵאָה in a pause is מָלֵאָה,
יִקְטְלוּ – וְקְטֹלוּ The vowel to be inserted depends on the
root of the word; for that vowel is restored which existed
in the root If there was no vowel in the root, Shevâ is
changed into Seghôl, v. g. שְבִר in a pause is שֶבֶר

Chapter II.
Etymology.

A. The verb.
I. The verb in general.
§ 21. Properties of Hebrew conjugations.

1 It is peculiar to the Hebrew, together with the other Semitic languages, that the primary notion of the verb is expressed in many more voices than in other languages This is effected by subjecting the root to various inflections which are called forms or classes, or even conjugations by ancient grammarians   We enumerate here the seven that are used more frequently, premising that their names, except the first, *Kal*, which signifies *light* (simple), are formed from the verb פָּעַל *he did.*

1. Kal (פָּעַל *he did*) primitive notion of the verb, v. g. *to kill.*
2. Niphal (נִפְעַל) is the passive of Kal: *to be killed;* sometimes reflexive: *to kill oneself.*
3. Piël (פִּעֵל) intensive or iterative: *to murder*
4. Pual (פֻּעַל), the passive of Piël: *to be murdered.*
5. Hiphil (הִפְעִיל) causative: *to cause to kill*
6. Hophal (הָפְעַל), the passive of Hiphil: *to be caused to kill* or *to be killed*
7. Hithpaël (הִתְפַּעֵל), reflexive and reciprocal: *to kill oneself* or *to kill one another.*

Note 1   Most Hebrew verbs are used in some of the seven conjugations only

2   There are many other forms of the verb, which, however, occur but seldom   We will indicate their form and signification at the end of § 32

2 The Hebrew has only two forms of tenses, the preterit and the future, or better the perfect and the imperfect

tenses; for they are not so much signs of past or future time, as of an action which is either completed or still going on. There is no proper and distinct form of the present tense Its idea is expressed by the participle or sometimes also by the imperfect and even the perfect tense

3. Properly speaking there is but one mode, the indicative Of the other quasi modes, the imperative can hardly be called a mode, the infinitive and participle are rather verbal nouns. The future is used for the subjunctive and the optative or jussive.

4. There are three persons, two numbers: the singular and the plural, and two genders, the masculine and feminine, which, however, have often a common form

§ 22. Construction of the forms of verbs.

1 There are two primitive forms of every verb: the third person singular of the perfect and the infinitive.

2 The other forms are derived from the primitive forms as from roots, partly by the addition of preformatives, partly of afformatives, partly by the mutation of the vowels, partly by the doubling of the middle consonant.

3. Preformatives are additions to the beginning, afformatives additions to the termination of the root

4 The primitive forms consist regularly of three consonants, which are the root or radical letters. Only a few verbs are quadriliteral

Note. The rules given in §§ 11—13 about the gutturals, the semivowels and the assimilation of consonants, produce a surprising variety of forms in the verbs Hence for the sake of perspicuity, verbs are divided into different classes according to the nature of their radicals. Thus we have first the firm verb which consists of mute consonants only and the weak (infirm) verb which contains semivowels. The firm verb undergoes some changes both on account of its having gutturals or letters which may be assimilated with others. Hence verbs are regular and irregular The irregular verbs are irregular because they are gutturals, or assimilative, or quiescent.

Paradigm of the regular verb;

		Kal		Niphal.	Piel
		Transitive	Intransitive		
Perf. sing. 3 *m.*		קָטַל	כָּבֵד	נִקְטַל	קִטֵּל
3. *f.*		קָטְלָה	כָּבְדָה	נקטלה	קִטְּלָה
2. *m.*		קָטַ֫לְתָּ	כָּבַ֫דְתָּ	נִקְטַ֫לְתָּ	קִטַּ֫לְתָּ
2. *f.*		קָטַלְתְּ	כָּבַדְתְּ	נקטלת	קִטַּלְתְּ
1. *c.*		קָטַ֫לְתִּי	כָּבַ֫דְתִּי	נִקְטַ֫לְתִּי	קִטַּ֫לְתִּי
plur. 3 *c.*		קָטְלוּ	כָּבְדוּ	נקטלו	קִטְּלוּ
2 *m.*		קְטַלְתֶּם	כבדתם	נִקְטַלְתֶּם	קִטַּלְתֶּם
2. *f.*		קְטַלְתֶּן	כבדתן	נְקְטַלְתֶּן	קִטַּלְתֶּן
1 *c.*		קָטַ֫לְנוּ	כָּבַ֫דְנוּ	נִקְטַ֫לְנוּ	קִטַּ֫לְנוּ

Inf. constr. קְטֹל (absol. קָטוֹל)	הִקָּטֵל (הִקָּטֹל)	קַטֵּל (קַטֹּל)

		Transitive	Intransitive	Niphal	Piel
Imp. sing. *m.*		קְטֹל	כְּבַד	הִקָּטֵל	קַטֵּל
f.		קִטְלִי	כִּבְדִי	הִקָּטְלִי	קַטְּלִי
plur. *m.*		קִטְלוּ	כִּבְדוּ	הִקָּטְלוּ	קַטְּלוּ
f.		קְטֹלְנָה	כְּבַ֫דְנָה	הִקָּטֹלְנָה	קַטֵּלְנָה

		Transitive	Intransitive	Niphal	Piel
Fut. sing. 3. *m.*		יִקְטֹל	יִכְבַּד	יִקָּטֵל	יְקַטֵּל
3. *f.*		תִּקְטֹל	תִּכְבַּד	תִּקָּטֵל	תְּקַטֵּל
2. *m.*		תִּקְטֹל	תִּכְבַּד	תִּקָּטֵל	תְּקַטֵּל
2. *f.*		תִּקְטְלִי	תִּכְבְּדִי	תִּקָּטְלִי	תְּקַטְּלִי
1 *c.*		אֶקְטֹל	אֶכְבַּד	אֶקָּטֵל	אֲקַטֵּל
plur. 3. *m.*		יִקְטְלוּ	יכבדו	יִקָּטְלוּ	יְקַטְּלוּ
3. *f.*		תִּקְטֹלְנָה	תִּכְבַּדְנָה	תִּקָּטֹלְנָה	תְּקַטֵּלְנָה
2. *m.*		תִּקְטְלוּ	תִּכְבְּדוּ	תִּקָּטְלוּ	תְּקַטְּלוּ
2. *f.*		תִּקְטֹלְנָה	תִּכְבַּדְנָה	תִּקָּטֵלְנָה	תְּקַטֵּלְנָה
1. *c.*		נִקְטֹל	נִכְבַּד	נִקָּטֵל	נְקַטֵּל

Particip.	act. קֹטֵל pass. קָטוּל	נִקְטָל	מְקַטֵּל

קָטַל *he killed.*

Pual.	Hiphil	Hophal.	Huhpael.
קֻטַּל	הִקְטִיל	הָקְטַל	הִתְקַטֵּל
קֻטְּלָה	הִקְטִילָה	הָקְטְלָה	הִתְקַטְּלָה
קֻטַּלְתָּ	הִקְטַלְתָּ	הָקְטַלְתָּ	הִתְקַטַּלְתָּ
קֻטַּלְת	הִקְטַלְת	הָקְטַלְת	הִתְקַטַּלְת
קֻטַּלְתִּי	הִקְטַלְתִּי	הָקְטַלְתִּי	הִתְקַטַּלְתִּי
קֻטְּלוּ	הִקְטִילוּ	הָקְטְלוּ	הִתְקַטְּלוּ
קֻטַּלְתֶּם	הִקְטַלְתֶּם	הָקְטַלְתֶּם	הִתְקַטַּלְתֶּם
קֻטַּלְתֶּן	הִקְטַלְתֶּן	הָקְטַלְתֶּן	הִתְקַטַּלְתֶּן
קֻטַּלְנוּ	הִקְטַלְנוּ	הָקְטַלְנוּ	הִתְקַטַּלְנוּ

Pual.	Hiphil	Hophal.	Huhpael.
	הָקְטֵל (הָקְטֵל) הַקְטִיל (הַקְטִיל) קְטֹל (קְטֹל)		הִתְקַטֵּל

	הַקְטֵל		הִתְקַטֵּל
	הַקְטִילִי		הִתְקַטְּלִי
	הַקְטִילוּ		הִתְקַטְּלוּ
	הַקְטֵלְנָה		הִתְקַטֵּלְנָה

Pual.	Hiphil	Hophal.	Huhpael.
יְקֻטַּל	יַקְטִיל (*)	יָקְטַל	יִתְקַטֵּל
תְּקֻטַּל	תַּקְטִיל	תָּקְטַל	תִּתְקַטֵּל
תְּקֻטַּל	תַּקְטִיל	תָּקְטַל	תִּתְקַטֵּל
תְּקֻטְּלִי	תַּקְטִילִי	תָּקְטְלִי	תִּתְקַטְּלִי
אֲקֻטַּל	אַקְטִיל	אָקְטַל	אֶתְקַטֵּל
יְקֻטְּלוּ	יַקְטִילוּ	יָקְטְלוּ	יִתְקַטְּלוּ
תְּקֻטַּלְנָה	תַּקְטֵלְנָה	תָּקְטַלְנָה	תִּתְקַטֵּלְנָה
תְּקֻטְּלוּ	תַּקְטִילוּ	תָּקְטְלוּ	תִּתְקַטְּלוּ
תְּקֻטַּלְנָה	תַּקְטֵלְנָה	תָּקְטַלְנָה	תִּתְקַטֵּלְנָה
נְקֻטַּל	נַקְטִיל	נָקְטַל	נִתְקַטֵּל

Pual.	Hiphil	Hophal.	Huhpael.
מְקֻטָּל	מַקְטִיל	מָקְטָל	מִתְקַטֵּל

*) יַקְטֵל *Futurum apocopatum*

II. The regular verb.

As פָּעַל ıs a guttural verb, we take as paradıgm
the regular verb קָטַל *he kılled*

§ 23. Formation of the perfect of the seven conjugations.

1 The first primitive form of the verb, that is, the 3. pers.
sing. of the preterıt or perfect Kal has Kamets under the
first radical (§ 18, 3), Pathach under the second if the verb
is transıtive; if intransitive, it often takes Tserê, sometimes
Chôlem (medial *e*, and medıal *o* verbs), v g. קָטַל *he kılled*,
כָּבֵד *he was heavy*, גָּדֹל *he was great*. The paradigm, therefore, begins with that person, since from ıt all the other
forms are derived

2 The remaining six conjugatıons are formed from
Kal, partly by means of preformatıves, partly by the change
of vowels, partly by the doublıng of the middle radical
These transformatıons are indicated by the very name of
the respective conjugations: as from פָּעַל we have נִפְעַל,
הפעיל etc, so from קָטַל we have נִקְטַל, הקטיל, etc

§ 24. Formation of the personal forms of the perfect.

1. As shown in the paradigms, the personal forms of
the verb with their gender and number are constıtuted by
the combination of old forms of the personal pronouns with
the root of the verb. The perfect Kal has these forms
joined to the root in the following manner:

Sing		Plur	
הָ—	III pers fem	וּ	III pers masc and fem.
תָּ	II pers. masc	תֶם	II pers. masc.
ת	II pers fem	תֶּן	II pers fem
תִי	I. pers. masc and fem	נוּ	I pers masc and fem.

In adding these afformatives to the root, § 19 about the elision of vowels is to be observed; hence before הָ—֖ and ֜ו the last vowel of the root is thrown out

2. According to the same rules the personal forms in all the seven conjugations are derived from the 3. pers. singular, except that a) the Chîrek magnum in Hiphil is not thrown out before an afformative beginning with a vowel (see § 19); b) that the long vowels of the last syllables in the conjugations Pièl, Hiphil and Hithpaèl are shortened when there is an accession of an afformative beginning with a consonant, and changed into Pathach, v. g. קָטַלְתָּ – קַטֵּל The same happens to Tserê and Chôlem in the intransitive conjugation of Kal, v g כָּבַדְתָּ – כָּבֵד. Consequently in all the forms of the perfect Pathach is the vowel of the last syllable of the root before afformatives that begin with a consonant.

§ 25. Infinitive and imperative.

1 The second primitive form of the verb is the infinitive construct It occurs in all the conjugations, and its form can be seen in the paradigms. There is, besides, another form of the infinitive, occurring less frequently, which has long vowels and is called the infinitive absolute.

2 The imperative has forms only for the 2ᵈ person singular and plural, masculine and feminine The 2 pers. masc. sing. does not differ from the infinitive construct; the other three are formed by means of the following afformatives:

יִ— fem sing, ֜ו masc. plur., נָה fem plur., and the elision of vowels in the fem sing. and the masc. plur. according to § 19 This elision causes one vocal Shᵉvâ to follow another, whence the first is changed into a Chîrek (see § 18) קִטְלִי, קִטְלוּ.

§ 26. Formation of the future and the participle.

1. The futures of all the conjugations are made by placing the ancient forms of the personal pronouns before the infinitive construct and adding, where necessary, the signs of the gender and number to the termination of the root. These twofold notes are:

Sing		Plur.	
3. m.	‫י—‬	‫י—ו (ון)‬	
3 f	‫ת—‬	‫ת—נָה‬	
2 m	‫ת—‬	‫ת—ו‬	
2. f (‫ין—‬) ‫ת—י‬		‫ת—נָה‬	
1. comm.	‫א—‬	‫נ—‬	

All these preformatives should per se have a vocal Shᵉvâ, which under the guttural ‫א‬ must be a Chateph. Hence where the infinitive construct begins with a vowelless consonant, the preformatives take Chîrek, except when there is a Chateph under the first radical; for then the preformative must take a corresponding vowel (§ 18, 2, b), v. g ‫יִקְטֹל – קְטֹל‬, ‫יַעֲמֹד – עֲמֹד; אֶקְטֹל‬. But where the preformatives are to precede *He*, the *He* is thrown out, and the preformatives take its place in regard to the vowel, v. g ‫יַקְטִיל‬ for ‫יְהַקְטִיל‬, ‫יָקְטַל‬ for ‫יְהָקְטַל‬. The afformatives added here follow the rules of § 19 on the elision of vowels.

2. The participle, except in Kal and Niphal which have different forms, is constructed in a similar way by prefixing ‫מ‬ to the root, and lengthening at the same time the Pathach in the second syllable, should it occur there. The participles of Kal are for transitive verbs, active ‫קֹטֵל‬, passive, also called *Paiul*, ‫קָטוּל‬; for intransitive verbs act ‫כָּבֵד‬ and ‫קָטֹן‬. The participle of Niphal differs from the perfect only by its lengthened vowel, v. g ‫נִקְטָל‬, ‫נִכְבָּד‬.

§ 27. The conversive Vav.

1 The perfect may be used in the sense of the imperfect or future, and the future in the sense of the perfect, if ו is placed before them, v g וְקָטַל he will kill, וַיִּקְטֹל he killed. This ו is called Vav conversive, because it converts or transforms the signification of the tenses It has two kinds of points: before the perfect it takes a simple Shᵉvâ; before the future a Pathach with a Daghesh-forte in the next letter, v g וְקָטַל, וַיִּקְטֹל (yet וָיִקְטֹל § 7, note, and וְאֶקְטֹל § 11, 2) These converted forms occur more frequently in Hebrew than the regular ones

2 The conversive Vav denotes ordinarily both a connection and a sequence, and is therefore also called Vav consecutive

3. In the converted future, the accent generally is thrown back to the preceding syllable, and the vowel of the last syllable, if a closed one, is shortened (§ 17, 1, a) v. g. יֹאמַר he will speak, וַיֹּאמֶר and he spoke, יָמֹת he will die, וַיָּמָת (vayyámŏth) and he died

§ 28. Subjunctive and jussive.

The Hebrews use the imperfect or future where the subjunctive would be required, v g יִגְמָר־נָא let it have an end, מִי יִדַּבֵּר who would have said? פֶּן־תְּכַחֵשׁוּ lest you lie (ne mentiamini) Likewise in the so called jussive mode they very frequently use the future or converted perfect, for the imperative, v. g לֹא תִגְנֹב thou shalt not steal, וְיָשַׁבְתָּ שָׁם (build a house) and dwell in it The proper forms of the imperative are but seldom used

ᵡ § 29. The paragogic form.

The vowel הָ— is appended to the first person, singular and plural, of the imperfect and to the second person

masc. of the imperative to bring into prominence the intention
of the speaker or writer, whence this *He* is called He para-
gogicum, that is intending   Thus שָׁמְרָה ,אֶזְכִּירָה ,אָקְטְלָה,
(shŏm‛râ), שׁכבָה. The future forms with this paragogic *He*
have a will-strengthening power, and are therefore also
called *Cohortative:* אשׁמְרָה *I shall beware,* נִדבְרָה *let us speak.*

When the paragogic *He* is affixed to a form, the last
vowel must be dropped, unless, as in Hiphil, it should be
fully written (§ 19)   Thus אָשְׁמְרָה comes from אָשְׁמֹר; but
אֲזכִּירָה from אֲזכִּיר

§ 30. The Daghesh-forte in the conjugations.

The three conjugations Piël, Pual and Hithpaèl have
the Daghesh-forte as a characteristic sign in the middle-
letter of the root, and may be thus distinguished by its
presence. The Niphal has it in its first radical in the infin,
imper and future

⌐ § 31. Future or imperfect of intransitive verbs.

The intransitive verbs which have Tserê or Chôlem in
the final syllable of the perfect, ordinarily take Pathach in
the future, v g. יגדַּל, יקטֹן   Sometimes there are two forms,
one with Chôlem, the other with Pathach, and in such a
case the first generally has a transitive, the second an intransitive signification, v. g. יטרֹף *he will despoil (somebody),*
יטרַף, *he will acquire spoils*

Note   Hence the name given by grammarians to the futures
in *O* and in *A*   They are both regular   The future in *E* occurs in
irregular verbs

⊬ § 32. The conjugation Hithpaël.

In verbs beginning with a sibilant (ז, ס, צ, שׂ, שׁ),
the Hithpaèl is formed by placing the ת of the preformative
after the first radical, v. g. שָׁבַת, Hithp. הִשׁתַּבֵּת, not
התשׁבֵּת   If the first radical is a צ, the ת is changed into ט, v. g.

צָדַק, Hithp הִצְטַדֵּק. Should the first radical be ד or ט or ת,
the ת of the preformative is assimilated with it, v. g דָּבַר,
Hithp הִדַּבֵּר, טָמֵא, Hithp הִטַּמֵּא, תָּמַם, Hithp הִתַּמֵּם

Note   Rare forms of verbs to which we alluded § 21 note 2
are the following, as framed on the verb *katal*·

Kôtel like *katal* but always transitive, *Kôtal*, passive; *kitlal* and
its passive *kutlal*; *k^etaltal* and its passive *k^o taltal* have an augmenting
power; *tiktel; hithkôtel*, reciprocal and passive; *hithkatlel* (not *hith-kattel*); *kilkel* signifying promptly repeated actions; *kolkal*, passive;
hithkalkel, reflexive

The conjugations of all these forms are inflected according to
the paradigms of the others. Their exact signification is often to
be furnished by the context

III. The irregular verbs.

A. The guttural verbs.

If one of the three radicals is a guttural or a ר, some peculiar
forms arise in their conjugations (§ 11) These will be more clearly
described by dividing the guttural verbs into verbs of the first gut-tural, of the second and of the third guttural, according to the
respective place that the guttural occupies in the root

Note   Some grammars call these verbs also Pê guttural, 'Ayin
guttural and Lamedh guttural according to the system explained in
the note preceding § 36 (below)

§ 33. Verbs of the first guttural.

When the first radical is a guttural, those forms appear
irregular in which the first radical should have a simple
Sh^evâ; for according to § 11, 1, that Sh^evâ must be a
Chateph, at least where the Sh^evâ should be vocal   This
occurs in the infin and imper and future of Kal, in the
perfect of Niphal, and in the whole of Hiphil and Hophal.
In the future of Kal, in the perfect of Niphal, in Hiphil,
where the Chîrek of the preformative was produced from
a vocal Sh^evâ, the rules given § 18, 2, *b* are observed.
Where the silent Sh^evâ is retained (§ 11, 1), the vowel of

the preformative is still selected as if the guttural had a Chateph, v. g. הָהֻפַּךְ, יַחֲשִׁיךְ, נֶעְדַּר, יֵחֹבַט, יֵחְדַּל (*hŏhpach*).

The rule, forbidding gutturals to receive a Daghesh, affects the infin., imper., future of Niphal, the forms of which are constructed according to §§ 11, 2 and 17, 2, *b*.

Note. The future of the Intransitives in *A* (§ 31) ordinarily selects the Chateph-seghôl for its preformatives, v g יֶחֱזַק *he will be strong*, and the same Chateph is not unfrequently used for Chateph-pathach in the imperfect of transitive verbs, especially if these begin with א, v g יֶחְשֹׁף *he will uncover*, יֶאֱסֹף *he will gather*.

Paradigm of the verb of the first guttural;
עָמַד *he stood*, חָזַק *he was strong*.

		Kal.		Niphal.	Hiphil.	Hophal
Perf. sing. 3 m.		עָמַד		נֶעֱמַד	הֶעֲמִיד	הָעֳמַד
3 f.		עָמְדָה		נֶעֶמְדָה	הֶעֱמִידָה	הָעָמְדָה
2 m.		עָמַ֫דְתָּ		נֶעֱמַדְתָּ	הֶעֱמַ֫דְתָּ	הָעֳמַדְתָּ
2 f.		עָמַדְתּ		נֶעֱמַדְתּ	הֶעֱמַדְתּ	הָעָמַדְתּ
1 c.		עָמַ֫דְתִּי		נֶעֱמַ֫דְתִּי	הֶעֱמַ֫דְתִּי	הָעֳמַ֫דְתִּי
plur. 3 c.		עָמְדוּ		נֶעֶמְדוּ	הֶעֱמִידוּ	הָעָמְדוּ
2 m.		עֲמַדְתֶּם		נֶעֱמַדְתֶּם	הֶעֱמַדְתֶּם	הָעֳמַדְתֶּם
2 f.		עֲמַדְתֶּן		נֶעֱמַדְתֶּן	הֶעֱמַדְתֶּן	הָעָמַדְתֶּן
1 c		עָמַ֫דְנוּ		נֶעֱמַ֫דְנוּ	הֶעֱמַ֫דְנוּ	הָעֳמַ֫דְנוּ
Inf. absol.		עָמוֹד		נַעֲמוֹד	הַעֲמֵיד	
constr.		עֲמֹד		הֵעָמֵד	הַעֲמִיד	הָעֳמַד
Imp. sing. m.		עֲמֹד	חֲזַק	הֵעָמֵד	הַעֲמֵד	
f.		עִמְדִי	חִזְקִי	הֵעָמְדִי	הַעֲמִ֫ידִי	
plur. m.		עִמְדוּ	חִזְקוּ	הֵעָמְדוּ	הַעֲמִ֫ידוּ	
f.		עֲמֹ֫דְנָה	חֲזַ֫קְנָה	הֵעָמַ֫דְנָה	הַעֲמֵ֫דְנָה	
Fut. sing. 3 m.		יַעֲמֹד	יֶחֱזַק	יֵעָמֵד	יַעֲמִיד	יָעֳמַד
3 f.		תַּעֲמֹד	תֶּחֱזַק	תֵּעָמֵד	תַּעֲמִיד	תָּעֳמַד
2 m.		תַּעֲמֹד	תֶּחֱזַק	תֵּעָמֵד	תַּעֲמִיד	תָּעֳמַד
2 f.		תַּעַמְדִי	תֶּחֶזְקִי	תֵּעָמְדִי	תַּעֲמִ֫ידִי	תָּעָמְדִי
1 c.		אֶעֱמֹד	אֶחֱזַק	אֵעָמֵד	אַעֲמִיד	אָעֳמַד

Verbs of the second guttural. 31

		Kal		Niphal	Hiphil	Hophal
plur	3 m.	יַעֲמֹדוּ	יַחְזְקוּ	יֵעָמְדוּ	יַעֲמִידוּ	יָעֳמְדוּ
	3 f.	תַּעֲמֹדְנָה	תֶּחֱזַקְנָה	תֵּעָמֹדְנָה	תַּעֲמֵדְנָה	תָּעֳמַדְנָה
	2 m	תַּעַמְדוּ	תֶּחֶזְקוּ	תֵּעָמְדוּ	תַּעֲמִידוּ	תָּעֳמְדוּ
	2 f	תַּעֲמֹדְנָה	תֶּחֱזַקְנָה	תֵּעָמֹדְנָה	תַּעֲמֵדְנָה	תָּעֳמַדְנָה
	1 c.	נַעֲמֹד	נֶחֱזַק	נֵעָמֵד	נַעֲמִיד	נָעֳמַד

Fut apoc				יַעֲמֵד	
Part. act.	עֹמֵד		נֶעֱמָד	מַעֲמִיד	מָעֳמָד
pass.	עָמוּד				

The forms Piël, Pual and Hithpaël are omitted because they have no irregularities on account of the guttural.

✗ § 34. Verbs of the second guttural.

These verbs are irregular in Piël, Pual and Hithpaël according to the rule of § 11, 2, especially for the letter ר. Where the middle radical is ה or ח, the implicit Daghesh-forte is admitted, and the vowels remain short, v. g כִּחֵד, בֵּהֵל, רִחַם. The future Kal of all these verbs takes the vowel A (§ 11, 3) For the simple Sheʿvâ the guttural requires a Chateph, v. g שָׁחֲטוּ, יִשְׁחֲטוּ; the Imper שַׁחֲטִי is according to § 18, 2, b

Paradigm of the verb of the second guttural
זָעַק he clamored, בָּרַךְ he knelt.

		Kal.	Niphal.	Piel.	Pual.	Hithpael.
Perf. sing.	3 m.	זָעַק	נזעק	בֵּרֵךְ	ברך	הִתְבָּרֵךְ
	3 f.	זָעֲקָה	נזעקה	בֵּרְכָה	בֹּרְכָה	הִתְבָּרְכָה
	2 m.	זָעַקְתָּ	נִזְעַקְתָּ	בֵּרַכְתָּ	בֹּרַכְתָּ	הִתְבָּרַכְתָּ
	2 f.	זָעַקְתְּ	נזעקת	בֵּרַכְתּ	בֹּרַכְתּ	הִתְבָּרַכְתּ
	1 c.	זָעַקְתִּי	נזעקתי	בֵּרַכְתִּי	בֹּרַכְתִּי	הִתְבָּרַכְתִּי
plur.	3 c.	זָעֲקוּ	נזעקו	ברכו	ברכו	הִתְבָּרְכוּ
	2 m.	זְעַקְתֶּם	נזעקתם	ברכתם	בֹּרַכְתֶּם	הִתְבָּרַכְתֶּם
	2 f.	זְעַקְתֶּן	נִזְעַקְתֶּן	בֵּרַכְתֶּן	בֹּרַכְתֶּן	הִתְבָּרַכְתֶּן
	1 c.	זָעַקְנוּ	נִזְעַקְנוּ	בֵּרַכְנוּ	בֹּרַכְנוּ	הִתְבָּרַכְנוּ

		Kal	Niphal.	Piel	Pual	Hithpael.
Inf. abs.		זָעוֹק	נזעוק	בָּרוֹךְ		
	constr.	זְעֹק	הִזָּעֵק	בָּרֵךְ	בֹּרַךְ	הִתבָּרֵךְ
Imp. sing. m.		זְעַק	הִזָּעֵק	בָּרֵךְ		הִתבָּרֵךְ
	f.	זַעֲקִי	הִזָּעֲקִי	בָּרְכִי		הִתבָּרְכִי
plur. m.		זַעֲקוּ	הִזָּעֲקוּ	בָּרְכוּ		הִתבָּרְכוּ
	f.	זְעַקְנָה	הִזָּעַקְנָה	בָּרֵכְנָה		הִתבָּרֵכְנָה
Fut. sing. 3 m.		יִזְעַק	יִזָּעֵק	יְבָרֵךְ	יְבֹרַךְ	יִתבָּרֵךְ
	3 f.	תִּזְעַק	תִּזָּעֵק	תְּבָרֵךְ	תְּבֹרַךְ	תִּתבָּרֵךְ
	2 m.	תִּזְעַק	תִּזָּעֵק	תְּבָרֵךְ	תְּבֹרַךְ	תִּתבָּרֵךְ
	2 f.	תִּזְעֲקִי	תִּזָּעֲקִי	תְּבָרְכִי	תְּבֹרְכִי	תִּתבָּרְכִי
	1 c.	אֶזְעַק	אֶזָּעֵק	אֲבָרֵךְ	אֲבֹרַךְ	אֶתבָּרֵךְ
plur. 3 m.		יזְעֲקוּ	יִזָּעֲקוּ	יְבָרְכוּ	יְבֹרְכוּ	יִתבָּרְכוּ
	3 f.	תִּזְעַקְנָה	תִּזָּעַקְנָה	תְּבָרֵכְנָה	תְּבֹרַכְנָה	תִּתבָּרֵכְנָה
	2 m.	תִּזְעֲקוּ	תִּזָּעֲקוּ	תְּבָרְכוּ	תְּבֹרְכוּ	תִּתבָּרְכוּ
	2 f.	תִּזְעַקְנָה	תִּזָּעַקְנָה	תְּבָרֵכְנָה	תְּבֹרַכְנָה	תִּתבָּרֵכְנָה
	3 c.	נִזְעַק	נִזָּעֵק	נְבָרֵךְ	נְבֹרַךְ	נִתבָּרֵךְ
Part. act.		זֹעֵק	נִזְעָק	מְבָרֵךְ	מְבֹרָךְ	מִתבָּרֵךְ
	pass.	זָעוּק				

§ 35. Verbs of the third guttural.

Those verbs only belong to this class which end in ה
or ח or ע; for א and ה at the end of words become
quiescent and lose their quality of consonants

The irregularity of these verbs results from the rules
laid down in § 11, 3; for hence spring the forms יִגְבַּה,
(פָּתְחָ) פָּתוּחַ, גָּבַהּ, הִרְשִׁיעַ, פָּתַח, שָׁמַע, פָּתַח etc. The guttural
admits a simple Sh°vâ, which, however, is changed into
Pathach in the 2ᵈ pers fem sing of the perfect in all the
conjugations, v. g. שָׁלַחַתּ for שָׁלַחְתּ (§ 18, 1, note 1).

B. Weak or infirm verbs.

Note   Those verbs are called weak or infirm that lose a vowel some way or other in their conjugation   This nearly always happens because formerly they consisted only of two letters   and received their third radical afterwards   This increment is either a semivowel or a Nûn; and as these may be located in various parts of the root, there arise various classes of weak verbs

To distinguish them, the grammarians, after the old paradigm פָּעַל, called the first radical of a verb פ, the second ע, the third ל, whence v. g   a verb Pê-Nûn (פֵּ״ן) is one whose first radical is נ, a verb Lamedh-He that whose last radical is ה   When, however, the second radical is doubled, the verb is called 'Ayin-'Ayin (ע״ע). In describing the peculiarities of these verbs, we follow the usage, which is not founded on logical sequence

§ 36. Verbs אֵּפ (Pê-'Aleph).

Five verbs beginning with א have this peculiarity that א in the future of Kal quiesces in Chôlem   They are: אָבַד *he perished*, אָבָה *he willed*, אָכַל *he ate*, אָמַר *he said*, אָפָה *he cooked*

These verbs, besides, as many others of the irregular classes, have in the last syllable of the future of Kal ordinarily Tserê, sometimes Pathach. This tense is therefore conjugated as follows:

Sing	Plur
יאמר (יֹאמַר)	יֹאמרו
תֹאמר	תֹּאמַרְנָה
תֹאמר	תֹּאמרו
תֹאמרי	תֹּאמַרְנָה
אמר (אֹמַר)	נֹאמַר

In the first pers   sing. where there should be two א, the second is assimilated, and so it writes אֹמַר, not אֹאמַר

The other forms of these verbs follow the rules of the first guttural verbs

Paradigm of the verb of the

			Kal.	*Niphal.*	*Piel*
Perf.	sing.	3. *m.*	שָׁלַח	נִשְׁלַח	שִׁלַּח
		3 *f.*	שָׁלְחָה	—	—
		2 *m.*	שָׁלַחְתָּ	—	—
		2 *f.*	שָׁלַחַתְּ	נִשְׁלַחַתְּ	שִׁלַּחַתְּ
			etc.		
Inf.	constr.		שְׁלֹחַ	הִשָּׁלַח	שַׁלַּח
	absol.		שָׁלוֹחַ	נִשְׁלֹחַ	שַׁלֵּחַ
Imp.	sing.	*m.*	שְׁלַח	הִשָּׁלַח	שַׁלַּח
		f.	שִׁלְחִי		
	plur.	*m.*	שִׁלְחוּ		
		f.	שְׁלַחְנָה		
Fut.	sing.	3. *m.*	יִשְׁלַח	יִשָּׁלַח	יְשַׁלַּח
		3. *f.*	תִּשְׁלַח	תִּשָּׁלַח	תְּשַׁלַּח
		2 *m.*	תִּשְׁלַח	תִּשָּׁלַח	תְּשַׁלַּח
		2. *f.*	תִּשְׁלְחִי	תִּשָּׁלְחִי	תְּשַׁלְּחִי
		1 *c.*	אֶשְׁלַח	אֶשָּׁלַח	אֲשַׁלַּח
	plur.	3. *m.*	יִשְׁלְחוּ	יִשָּׁלְחוּ	יְשַׁלְּחוּ
		3. *f.*	תִּשְׁלַחְנָה	תִּשָּׁלַחְנָה	תְּשַׁלַּחְנָה
		2. *m.*	תִּשְׁלְחוּ	תִּשָּׁלְחוּ	תְּשַׁלְּחוּ
		2. *f.*	תִּשְׁלַחְנָה	תִּשָּׁלַחְנָה	תְּשַׁלַּחְנָה
		1. *c.*	נִשְׁלַח	נִשָּׁלַח	נְשַׁלַּח
Part.	act.		שֹׁלֵחַ	נִשְׁלָח	מְשַׁלֵּחַ
	pass.		שָׁלוּחַ		

third guttural; שָׁלַח *he sent.*

Pual.	Hiphil.	Hophal.	Hithpael.
שֻׁלַּח	הִשְׁלִיחַ	הָשְׁלַח	הִשְׁתַּלַּח
—	הִשְׁלִיחָה	—	—
—	הִשְׁלַחְתְּ	—	—
שֻׁלַּחְתְּ	הִשְׁלַחְתְּ	הָשְׁלַחְתְּ	הִשְׁתַּלַּחְתְּ
שֻׁלַּח	הַשְׁלִיחַ	הָשְׁלַח	הִשְׁתַּלַּח
	הַשְׁלֵחַ	הָשְׁלַח	
	הַשְׁלֵחַ		הִשְׁתַּלֵּחַ
	הַשְׁלִיחִי		
	etc.		
יְשֻׁלַּח	(*יַשְׁלִיחַ	יָשְׁלַח	יִשְׁתַּלַּח
תְּשֻׁלַּח	תַּשְׁלִיחַ	תָּשְׁלַח	תִּשְׁתַּלַּח
תְּשֻׁלַּח	תַּשְׁלִיחַ	תָּשְׁלַח	תִּשְׁתַּלַּח
תְּשֻׁלְּחִי	תַּשְׁלִיחִי	תָּשְׁלְחִי	תִּשְׁתַּלְּחִי
אֲשֻׁלַּח	אַשְׁלִיחַ	אָשְׁלַח	אֶשְׁתַּלַּח
יְשֻׁלְּחוּ	יַשְׁלִיחוּ	יָשְׁלְחוּ	יִשְׁתַּלְּחוּ
תְּשֻׁלַּחְנָה	תַּשְׁלַחְנָה	תָּשְׁלַחְנָה	תִּשְׁתַּלַּחְנָה
תְּשֻׁלְּחוּ	תַּשְׁלִיחוּ	תָּשְׁלְחוּ	תִּשְׁתַּלְּחוּ
תְּשֻׁלַּחְנָה	תַּשְׁלַחְנָה	תָּשְׁלַחְנָה	תִּשְׁתַּלַּחְנָה
נְשֻׁלַּח	נַשְׁלִיחַ	נָשְׁלַח	נִשְׁתַּלַּח
מְשֻׁלָּח	מַשְׁלִיחַ	מָשְׁלָח	מִשְׁתַּלַּח

*) יַשְׁלַח Fut. apocop.

3*

§ 37. Verbs פֹּן (Pê-Nûn).

The verbs, whose first radical is נ, a) lose that נ in the imper and infin constr Kal, v. g. גַּשׁ from נָגַשׁ, גְּשׁוּ, נְשֶׁנָה; and b) where on account of a preformative the נ loses its vowel, it is assimilated by a Daghesh-forte with the following consonant, v. g ידר from נָדַר, אֶדֹּר, נִדַּר (Niph.) הִדִּיר, but then in Hophal it takes Kibbûts instead of Kamets-Chatuph, v g הֻדַּר, מֻדָּר. The rule therefore is that the Nûn which has a vocal Shᵉvâ (except נִדְרְתֶּם) is thrown out, but assimilated if it has a silent Shᵉvâ

The infinitive constr is ordinarily terminated by the syllable ת‍ֶ—, or, where a guttural occurs, ת‍ַ—, with the accent kept on the penult, v. g. נָגַשׁ, infin גֶּשֶׁת, נָגַע, infin גַּעַת. The remaining forms are regular

Paradigm of the verb Pê-Nûn; נָגַשׁ *he approached*

		Kal.	Niphal.	Hiphil.	Hophal.
Perf. sing. 3 *m.*		נָגַשׁ	נִגַּשׁ	הִגִּישׁ	הֻגַּשׁ
	3 *f.*	נָגְשָׁה	נִגְּשָׁה	הִגִּישָׁה	הֻגְּשָׁה
	2 *m.*	נָגַשְׁתָּ	נִגַּשְׁתָּ	הִגַּשְׁתָּ	הֻגַּשְׁתָּ
	2 *f.*	נָגַשְׁתְּ	נִגַּשְׁתְּ	הִגַּשְׁתְּ	הֻגַּשְׁתְּ
	1 *c*	נָגַשְׁתִּי	נִגַּשְׁתִּי	הִגַּשְׁתִּי	הֻגַּשְׁתִּי
plur. 3 *c*		נָגְשׁוּ	נִגְּשׁוּ	הִגִּישׁוּ	הֻגְּשׁוּ
	2 *m*	נְגַשְׁתֶּם	נִגַּשְׁתֶּם	הִגַּשְׁתֶּם	הֻגַּשְׁתֶּם
	2 *f*	נְגַשְׁתֶּן	נִגַּשְׁתֶּן	הִגַּשְׁתֶּן	הֻגַּשְׁתֶּן
	1 *c.*	נָגַשְׁנוּ	נִגַּשְׁנוּ	הִגַּשְׁנוּ	הֻגַּשְׁנוּ
Inf. absol		נָגוֹשׁ	הִנָּגֵשׁ	הַגֵּשׁ	
	constr.	גֶּשֶׁת	הִנָּגֵשׁ	הַגִּישׁ	הֻגַּשׁ

		Kal.	Niphal	Hiphil.	Hophal.
Imper. sing.	2 m.	גַּשׁ	הִגָּגֵשׁ	הַגֵּשׁ	
	2 f.	גְּשִׁי	הִגָּגְשִׁי	הַגִּישִׁי	
plur	2 m.	גְּשׁוּ	הִגָּגְשׁוּ	הַגִּישׁוּ	
	2 f.	גַּשְׁנָה	הִגָּגַשְׁנָה	הַגֵּשְׁנָה	
Fut. sing.	3 m.	יִגַּשׁ	יִגָּגֵשׁ	יַגִּישׁ	יֻגַּשׁ
	3 f.	תִּגַּשׁ	תִּגָּגֵשׁ	תַּגִּישׁ	תֻּגַּשׁ
	2 m.	תִּגַּשׁ	תִּגָּגֵשׁ	תַּגִּישׁ	תֻּגַּשׁ
	2 f.	תִּגְּשִׁי	תִּגָּגְשִׁי	תַּגִּישִׁי	תֻּגְּשִׁי
	1 c.	אֶגַּשׁ	אֶגָּגֵשׁ	אַגִּישׁ	אֻגַּשׁ
plur	3 m.	יִגְּשׁוּ	יִגָּגְשׁוּ	יַגִּישׁוּ	יֻגְּשׁוּ
	3 f	תִּגַּשְׁנָה	תִּגָּגַשְׁנָה	תַּגֵּשְׁנָה	תֻּגַּשְׁנָה
	2 m.	תִּגְּשׁוּ	תִּגָּגְשׁוּ	תַּגִּישׁוּ	תֻּגְּשׁוּ
	2 f.	תִּגַּשְׁנָה	תִּגָּגַשְׁנָה	תַּגֵּשְׁנָה	תֻּגַּשְׁנָה
	1 c.	נִגַּשׁ	נִגָּגֵשׁ	נַגִּישׁ	נֻגַּשׁ
Fut. apoc.				יַגֵּשׁ	
Part. act.		נֹגֵשׁ	נִגָּשׁ	מַגִּישׁ	מֻגָּשׁ
pass.		נָגֹשׁ			

The verbs Pê-Nûn can be known by the Daghesh-forte which they have in the first radical after a preformative

Note 1 The Nûn is not ordinarily assimilated with a following guttural v g נָחַת, מַנְחִיל; yet we have the Niphal נִחַם according to § 11, 2

2 The verb נָתַן *he gave,* has, besides the anomalies of the verbs פ"ן, also this peculiarity that the third radical נ is assimilated with a following ת, v g 2 pers sing perf נָתַתָּ for נָתַנְתָּ and the infin תֵּת for תֵּנְת (Also תְּנָה for נָתְנָה Ps VIII, 2) The last vowel of the future is E (יִתֵּן)

3 The verb לָקַח *he took* follows the rules of the verbs פ"ן in regard to its ל, except in Niphal Thus future יִקַּח, infin קַחַת, imperf Hophal יֻקַּח, but נִלְקַח

§ 38. Verbs פֿ״י (Pê-Yôdh).

The verbs, whose first radical is י, are divided into three classes:

1 The first class (called פֿ״י contracted verbs) consists of verbs whose first radical follows the rules of the פֿ״ן verbs, viz. יָצַת he burned (Niph. נִצַּת, Hiph הִצִּית, יָצַע he placed under, יָצַק he poured out, יָצַר he formed (all with second radical צ)

2 The second class of פֿ״י verbs, the only one which properly belongs here, has only this peculiarity that Yôdh in the future of Kal and in Hiphil becomes quiescent in the vowel of the preformative (§ 12), the former being Chîrek, the latter Tserê. All the rest is alike for these verbs and those of the third class, of which presently Thus יָטַב has the imperf יִיטַב, perf Hiph הֵיטִיב, future Hiph. יֵיטִיב.

Six verbs constitute this second class: יָצַר he formed, יָשַׁר he was right, יָטַב he was good, יָנַק he sucked, יָלַל he lamented, יָקַץ he awoke

Note These verbs have nearly always the imper and the future in A The infin of Kal is generally regular

3 The third class comprises the verbs פֿ״י not yet described They were formerly פֿ״ו, a fact which explains most of their anomalies

4. These verbs take back their original ו in stead of י in Niphal, Hiphil and Hophal. Hence in these three conjugations we do not find the usual auxiliary vowel, but in its place another vowel that is homogenous to Vav. Thus Niphal (in perfect) and Hiphil take a Chôlem in which Vav quiesces, and Hophal takes Shûrek, v g Kal יָצַר, Niph. נוֹצַר, Hiph הוֹצִיר, Hoph הוּצַר; נוֹסַף, הוֹאִיל, הוֹלִיד, יוֹלִיד, אוּבְרִישׁ, אוּכַל.

5. In the infin, imper and future Niphal the letter Yôdh is simply replaced by the consonant Vav; infin. הִוָּצֵר, imperf יִוָּצֵר.

Paradigm of the verbs פ״ו (3 cl פו״);
יָצַר (1. and 2. cl.) *he formed;* (3. cl.) *he was pressed.*

	Kal.	Niphal.	Hiphil	Hophal
Perf.	יָצַר	נוֹצַר	הוֹצִיר	הוּצַר
	יָצְרָה	נוֹצְרָה	הוֹצִירָה	הוּצְרָה
	etc.	נוֹצַרְתָּ	הוֹצַרְתָּ	הוּצַרְתָּ
	regul.	נוֹצַרְתְּ	הוֹצַרְתְּ	הוּצַרְתְּ
		נוֹצַרְתִּי	הוֹצַרְתִּי	הוּצַרְתִּי
		נוֹצְרוּ	הוֹצִירוּ	הוּצְרוּ
		נוֹצַרְתֶּם	הוֹצַרְתֶּם	הוּצַרְתֶּם
		נוֹצַרְתֶּן	הוֹצַרְתֶּן	הוּצַרְתֶּן
		נוֹצַרְנוּ	הוֹצִירְנוּ	הוּצַרְנוּ
Inf. constr.	צָרָת	הִוָּצֵר	הוֹצִיר	הוּצַר
absol.	יָצוֹר		הוֹצֵר	
Imp.	צַר יְצַר	הִוָּצֵר	הוֹצֵר	
	צְרִי יַצְרִי	הִוָּצְרִי	הוֹצִירִי	
	צְרוּ יַצְרוּ	הִוָּצְרוּ	הוֹצִירוּ	
	צֵרְנָה יַצֵּרְנָה	הִוָּצֵרְנָה	הוֹצֵרְנָה	
Futur.	יְצַר	יִוָּצֵר	יוֹצִיר	יוּצַר
	תֵּצַר	תִּוָּצֵר	תּוֹצִיר	תּוּצַר
	תֵּצַר	תִּוָּצֵר	תּוֹצִיר	תּוּצַר
	תֵּצְרִי	תִּוָּצְרִי	תּוֹצִירִי	תּוּצְרִי
	אֵצַר	אִוָּצֵר	אוֹצִיר	אוּצַר
	יְצְרוּ	יִוָּצְרוּ	יוֹצִירוּ	יוּצְרוּ
	תֵּצֵרְנָה	תִּוָּצֵרְנָה	תּוֹצִירְנָה	תּוּצַרְנָה
	תֵּצְרוּ	תִּוָּצְרוּ	תּוֹצִירוּ	תּוּצְרוּ
	תֵּצֵרְנָה	תִּוָּצֵרְנָה	תּוֹצֵרְנָה	תּוּצַרְנָה
	נֵצַר	נִוָּצֵר	נוֹצִיר	נוּצַר
Part. act. יֹצֵר pass. יָצוּר		נוֹצָר	מוֹצִיר	מוּצָר

6 In the future of Kal the first radical is entirely omitted, and the preformative, making an open syllable, receives Tserê: יֵצֵר, יֵדְעוּ.

7. The infinitive, and nearly always the imperative, is formed the same way as the infinitive of the verbs פֿ̎ן: the Yôdh is omitted, and the infinitive ends in the syllable תֿ— or תֿ—֗; v. g יָצֵר, imper. צֵר (יְצֵר), infin. צֶרֶת; יְדַע, infin. דַעַת (see § 37)

Note. The forms of the 3 class, which is very numerous, are given in full; the other two, where they differ from the third, are indicated by their chief form in the side lines.

Note 1. The verbs פֿ̎י of the 3. class have ordinarily their future in E; but when there is a guttural in the second syllable they take A, v. g. יֵרַד, תֵּרַד.

2. There are Pê-Yôdh verbs that belong to more than one class, v g. יָשַׁר, fut. יִישַׁר and יִשַׁר; יָבֵשׁ, fut ייבַשׁ, Hiph חוֹבִישׁ; יָלַד, fut יוֹלִיד, infin Hoph חֻלְדָת

3 The verb הָלַךְ he went was formerly יָלַךְ This is the reason why the forms derived from the latter root are more in use in all the conjugations and tenses, except the perfect, participle and infinitive absolute of Kal: thus Kal infin constr לֶכֶת, imper לֵךְ, fut יֵלֵךְ, perf Hiph חוֹלִיךְ, etc.

§ 39. Verbs עֵ (double 'Ayin).

The verbs עֵ have peculiar inflections because, as often as it is possible, the second radical is contracted with the third. Therefore like the 2. class of the פֿ̎י they are called contracted verbs

1 The second radical does not combine with the third, where the vowels cannot be thrown out, that is in the infin. absol. and the participle of Kal, and in the three conjugations Poël, Poal and Hithpoël (for reason and formation of which see n 6 below) Everywhere else the doubled letter is written only once, but marked, when

allowed, with a Daghesh-forte In this manner the verb
becomes monosyllabic The Daghesh, not being admitted in
a final consonant (§ 7, note 1), appears only in the forms
which are augmented by an afformative; v g sing Kal 3. m.
סַב, 3 f סָבְה.

2 The root, thus made a monosyllable, is noted everywhere with that vowel which the same form of the regular
verb has in the last syllable of the root, v. g סַב (סָבַב),
imper. סֹב (סבב); except, however, the infin and the future
of Niphal, which have Pathach instead of Tserê: הַסַב for
הִסָבֵב; יִסַב for יִסָבֵב, and Hiphil with Tserê instead of Chîrek,
חֵסֵב instead of הַסִביב.

3. The preformatives of the monosyllabic root have
long vowels, because their syllables are open Thus in the
perfect Niphal and the imperfect of Kal they have Kamets:
future Kal יָסֹב, Niph. נָסַב; but in Hiph הֵסַב (part. מֵסֵב),
in Hoph הוּסַב.

4 In all forms whose afformative begins with a consonant, the syllable with its Daghesh-forte would close with
two consonants, which is contrary to § 18, 1. This is why
before those afformatives the grammar requires an auxiliary
vowel, which is a full Chôlem in the perfect, a Seghôl with
a quiescent Yôdh in the future and imper., v g סַבּוֹת and
תְּסֻבֶּינָה As these new vowels take the accent, the Kamets,
which according to the rule precedes an accented syllable
(§ 18, 3), is thrown out, v. g. Niph. נְסַב (for נסב), 2. m.
becomes נְסַבּוֹת; likewise תְּסֻבֶּינָה and תְּסֻבֶּינָה.

5 The vowels are shortened, as is shown in the paradigm, in imper. and future of Kal (imper. 2 fem plur. סֻבֶּינָה,
future 2. and 3. fem. plur תְּסֻבֶּינָה) and in Hiphil (perf. 3.
sing הֵסַב, 2. masc. הֲסִבּוֹתָ, etc imperf. יָסֵב, 2. and 3. fem.
plur. תְּסֻבֶּינָה). This abbreviation is effected by transferring
the accent to the auxiliary vowel (§ 17, 1 a) Yet, contrary
to this rule, the accent is not transferred to the afformatives

Paradigm of the verb עע ('Ayin-'Ayin);

	Kal		Niphal.	Poël.
Perf. sing. 3 m.	סַב		נָסַב	סוֹבֵב
3 f.	סָבָה		נָסַבָּה	סוֹבְבָה
2 m.	סַבּוֹתָ		נְסַבּוֹתָ	סוֹבַבְתָּ
2 f	סַבּוֹת		נְסַבּוֹת	סוֹבַבְתְּ
1 c.	סַבּוֹתִי		נְסַבּוֹתִי	סוֹבַבְתִּי
plur. 3 c	סַבּוּ		נָסַבּוּ	סוֹבְבוּ
2 m.	סַבּוֹתֶם		נְסַבּוֹתֶם	סוֹבַבְתֶּם
2 f	סַבּוֹתֶן		נְסַבּוֹתֶן	סוֹבַבְתֶּן
1 c.	סַבּוֹנוּ		נְסַבּוֹנוּ	סוֹבַבְנוּ
Inf. absol.	סָבוֹב		הִסּוֹב	
constr.	סֹב		הִסַּב י	סוֹבֵב
Imper. sing. m.	סֹב		הִסַּב	סוֹבֵב
f.	סֹבִּי		הִסַּבִּי	סוֹבְבִי
plur. m.	סֹבּוּ		הִסַּבּוּ	סוֹבְבוּ
f.	סֻבֶּינָה		הִסַּבֶּינָה	סוֹבֵבְנָה
Fut. sing. 3 m.	יָסֹב	יִסֹּב	יִסַּב	יְסוֹבֵב
3 f.	תָּסֹב	תִּסֹּב	תִּסַּב	תְּסוֹבֵב
2 m.	תָּסֹב	תִּסֹּב	תִּסַּב	תְּסוֹבֵב
2 f.	תָּסֹבִּי	תִּסֹּבִּי	תִּסַּבִּי	תְּסוֹבְבִי
1 c.	אָסֹב	אֶסֹּב	אֶסַּב	אֲסוֹבֵב
plur. 3 m.	יָסֹבּוּ	יִסֹּבּוּ	יִסַּבּוּ	יְסוֹבְבוּ
3 f.	תָּסֻבֶּינָה	תִּסֹּבְנָה	תִּסַּבֶּינָה	תְּסוֹבֵבְנָה
2 m.	תָּסֹבּוּ	תִּסֹּבּוּ	תִּסַּבּוּ	תְּסוֹבְבוּ
2 f.	תָּסֻבֶּינָה	תִּסֹּבְנָה	תִּסַּבֶּינָה	תְּסוֹבֵבְנָה
1 c.	נָסֹב	נִסֹּב	נִסַּב	נְסוֹבֵב
Fut. convers.	וַיָּסָב (vayyásobh)			
Fut. with suffix.	יְסֻבֵּנִי			יְסוֹבְבֵנִי
Part. act.	סוֹבֵב		נָסָב	מְסוֹבֵב
pass.	סָבוּב			

סַב *he turned*

Poal.	Hiphil	Hophal	Hithpoel.
סוֹבֵב	הֵסַב	הוּסַב	הִסְתּוֹבֵב
סוֹבְבָה	הֵסַבָּה	הוּסַבָּה	הִסְתּוֹבְבָה
סוֹבַּתָ	הֲסִבּוֹתָ	הוּסַבּוֹתָ	הִסְתּוֹבַבְתָ
סוּבַּבְתְ	הֲסִבּוֹת	הוּסַבּוֹת	הִסְתּוֹבַבְתְ
סוֹבַּבְתִּי	הֲסִבּוֹתִי	הוּסַבּוֹתִי	הִסְתּוֹבַבְתִּי
סוֹבְבוּ	הֵסַבּוּ	הוּסַבּוּ	הִסְתּוֹבְבוּ
סוֹבַבְתֶּם	הֲסִבּוֹתֶם	הוּסַבּוֹתֶם	הִסְתּוֹבַבְתֶּם
סוֹבַבְתֶּן	הֲסִבּוֹתֶן	הוּסַבּוֹתֶן	הִסְתּוֹבַבְתֶּן
סוֹבַּבְנוּ	הֲסִבּוֹנוּ	הוּסַבּוֹנוּ	הִסְתּוֹבַבְנוּ
סוֹבֵב	הָסֵב	הוּסַב	הָסְתּוֹבב
	הָסֵב		הִסְתּוֹבֵב
	הָסֵבִּי		הִסְתּוֹבְבִי
	הָסֵבּוּ		הִסְתּוֹבְבוּ
	הָסְבֶּינָה		הִסְתּוֹבְבנָה
יְסוֹבַב	יָסֵב	יוּסַב	יִסְתּוֹבֵב
תְּסוֹבַב	תָּסֵב	תּוּסַב	תִּסְתּוֹבֵב
תְּסוֹבַב	תָּסֵב	תּוּסַב	תִּסְתּוֹבֵב
תְּסוֹבְבִי	תָּסֵבִּי	תּוּסַבִּי	תִּסְתּוֹבְבִי
אֲסוֹבַב	אָסֵב	אוּסַב	אֶסְתּוֹבֵב
יְסוֹבְבוּ	יָסֵבּוּ	יוּסַבּוּ	יִסְתּוֹבְבוּ
תְּסוֹבַבְנָה	תְּסֻבֶּינָה	תּוּסַבֶּינָה	תִּסְתּוֹבַבְנָה
תְּסוֹבְבוּ	תָּסֵבּוּ	תּוּסַבּוּ	תִּסְתּוֹבְבוּ
תְּסוֹבַבְנָה	תְּסֻבֶּינָה	תּוּסַבֶּינָה	תִּסְתּוֹבַבְנָה
נְסוֹבַב	נָסֵב	נוּסַב	נִסְתּוֹבֵב
	וַיָּסֵב		
	יְסֻבֵּנִי יְסֻבְּכֶם		
מְסוֹבַב	מֵסֵב	מוּסַב	מִסְתּוֹבֵב

הָ—ֵ, רְ, —ֵר of these verbs, and in Hiphil the vowel before them remains long, v. g perf. 3. fem sing. הֵסַבָּה, 3. masc. plur. הֵסֵבּוּ, imperf 2. fem sing תָּסֹבִּי

6. New conjugations. — In Piël, Pual and Hithpaël of these verbs, the second radical, doubled according to rule, would appear three times in succession. To obviate this incongruity, three new conjugations Poël, Poal and Hithpoël were formed, which are inflected like the regular verb. Some verbs even double their monosyllabic root and thus produce the conjugations that are called Pilpel and Hithpalpel, v. g. גִּלְגֵּל *he rolled*, Hithpalpel הִתְגַּלְגֵּל *he rolled himself*, from the root גָּלַל.

§ 40. Verbs עֹוּ ('Ayin-Vav).

To this class belong the verbs, whose middle radical seems to have been ו, while this letter is now either omitted or changed into וֹ or ו. Their inflection offers more and greater anomalies than any of the preceding classes. To unterstand their forms it will be of great help to compare these 'Ayin-Vav verbs with the preceding 'Ayin-'Ayin.

Note The עֹוּ verbs are always quoted in the infinitive, because thus they are more easily distinguished from the עֹ

I The verbs עֹוּ as קוּם have certain features in common with the עֹ verbs as סַב, viz.

1. that the root has only two letters and is a monosyllable;

2. that the preformatives have long vowels, and namely Kamets in the future Kal and in the perfect Niphal (very rarely Tserê, which, however, they have always in the perf. and partic Hiph. מֵקִים, הֵקִים);

3. that instead of Piël, Poal and Hithp they have the forms Polel, Polal and Hithpolel (הִתְקוֹמֵם, קוֹמֵם, קוֹמֵם) equivalent to the forms Poël, Poal and Hithpoël of the verbs עֹ;

4 that there is also an auxiliary vowel, וֹ in the perf,
־ֶ in the future, before afformatives beginning with a consonant (this, however, occurs only in the future Kal and
in the perf Niphal and Hiphil, not in the perf Kal or in
the future Niph or Hiph nor in all Hophal), v g future
Kal 3. f. plur תְּקוּמֶֽינָה, Niph perf 2 m sing. נְקוּמֹֽותָ,
Hiph perf 2. m sing הֲקִימֹֽותָ, but perf Kal 2. m. קַֽמְתָּ.

Note Before the afformative נָה in the future Niph וֹ is changed
into ־ֹ, in the future Hiph ־ֶי into ־ֶ, v g תָּקֹמְנָה, תְּקִמֶֽנָה

II. The verb קוּם has a punctuation of the monosyllabic
root, different from the verb סַב, in the following manner:

1 The perfect has Kamets or in the intransitives also
Tserê and Chôlem, v g קָם, מֵת (from מוּת), אוֹר;

2. the imper, infin, future and partic pass Kal have
Shûrek or Chôlem: imper. and infin קוּם, בוֹא, future יָקוּם,
יָבוֹא, partic pass לוֹט;

3. the future convers. of Kal has Kamets-chatûph, sometimes Kibbûts, v g וַיָּֽקָם, וַיָּֽלֶם;

4. the partic act has Kamets, or also in the intransitives
Tserê: קָם, מֵת;

5. the whole Niphal has Chôlem, which is changed into
Shûrek, when the accent is transferred: perf נָקוֹם, נְקוּמוֹת,
imperf. יִקּוֹם;

6. Hiphil keeps the Chîrek magnum: perf הֵקִים, imperf
יָקִים, apoc imperf יָקֶם, וַיָּֽקֶם.

Note Not all verbs whose medial letter is וֹ are irregular, for
in some the Vav retains the power of a consonant, especially in all
those whose last radical is He, v g צָוָה, Piel צִוָּה he commanded;
קָוָה, Piel קִוָּה he expected, also גָּוַע, imperf יִגְוַע he expired

§ 41. Verbs עֵ ('Ayin-Yôdh)

Some verbs of the foregoing class, besides the forms
we have described, have, as will be seen in the paradigm, in
the whole of Kal, except the partic, a second form, which
is marked with the Chîrek gadhol, whence they are named

Paradigm of the verbs ע"ו and ע"י;

	Kal.	Niphal	Hiphil.	Hophal.
Perf. sing. 3 *m.*	קָם	נָקוֹם	הֵקִים	הוּקַם
3. *f.*	קָ֫מָה	נָק֫וֹמָה	הֵקִ֫ימָה	הוּקְמָה
2. *m.*	קַ֫מְתָּ	נְקוּמ֫וֹתָ	הֲקִימ֫וֹתָ	הוּקַ֫מְתָּ
2. *f.*	קַמְתְּ	נְקוּמוֹת	הֲקִימוֹת	הוּקַמְתְּ
1. *c.*	קַ֫מְתִּי	נְקוּמ֫וֹתִי	הֲקִימ֫וֹתִי	הוּקַ֫מְתִּי
plur. 3. *c.*	קָ֫מוּ	נָק֫וֹמוּ	הֵקִ֫ימוּ	הוּקְמוּ
2. *m.*	קַמְתֶּם	נְקוּמוֹתֶם	הֲקִימוֹתֶם	הוּקַמְתֶּם
2. *f.*	קַמְתֶּן	נְקוּמוֹתֶן	הֲקִימוֹתֶן	הוּקַמְתֶּן
1. *c.*	קַ֫מְנוּ	נְקוּמ֫וֹנוּ	הֲקִימ֫וֹנוּ	הוּקַ֫מְנוּ
Inf. constr.	קוּם (*abs.* קוֹם)	הִקּוֹם הֵקוֹם	הָקִים (הָקֵם / הָקֵים)	הוּקַם
Imp. sing. m.	קוּם	הִקּוֹם	הָקֵם	
f.	ק֫וּמִי	הִקּ֫וֹמִי	הָקִ֫ימִי	
plur. m.	ק֫וּמוּ	הִקּ֫וֹמוּ	הָקִ֫ימוּ	
f.	קֹ֫מְנָה	הִקֹּ֫מְנָה	הָקֵ֫מְנָה	
Fut. sing. 3. *m.*	יָקוּם	יִקּוֹם	יָקִים	יוּקַם
3. *f.*	תָּקוּם	תִּקּוֹם	תָּקִים	תּוּקַם
2 *m.*	תָּקוּם	תִּקּוֹם	תָּקִים	תּוּקַם
2. *f.*	תָּק֫וּמִי	תִּקּ֫וֹמִי	תָּקִ֫ימִי	תּוּקְמִי
1. *c.*	אָקוּם	אֶקּוֹם	אָקִים	אוּקַם
plur. 3 *m.*	יָק֫וּמוּ	יִקּ֫וֹמוּ	יָקִ֫ימוּ	יוּקְמוּ
3. *f*	תְּקוּמֶ֫ינָה	תִּקֹּ֫מְנָה	תָּקֵ֫מְנָה	תּוּקַמְנָה
2. *m.*	תָּק֫וּמוּ	תִּקֹּ֫מוּ	תָּקִ֫ימוּ	תּוּקְמוּ
2. *f.*	תְּקוּמֶ֫ינָה	תִּקֹּ֫מְנָה	תָּקֵ֫מְנָה	תּוּקַמְנָה
1. *c.*	נָקוּם	נִקּוֹם	נָקִים	נוּקַם
Fut. apoc.	יָקֹם		יָקֵם	
conv.	וַיָּ֫קָם, וַיָּקָם		וַיָּ֫קֶם	
Fut. cum suff.	יְקִימֵ֫נִי		יְקִימֵ֫נִי	
Part.	קָם (*pass.* קוּם)	נָקוֹם	מֵקִים	מוּקָם

קוּם *he arose*; בִּין *he understood*.

Polel (Pilel).	Poïal (Pulal).	Kal		Niphal.
קוֹמֵם	קוֹמַם	בָּן	בִּין	נָבוֹן
קוֹמְמָה	קוֹמְמָה	בָּנָה	בִּינָה	נָבוֹנָה
קוֹמַ֫מְתָּ	קוֹמַ֫מְתָּ	בַּ֫נְתָּ	בִּינוֹתָ	נבונותָ
קוֹמַ֫מְתְּ	קוֹמַ֫מְתְּ	בַּנְתְּ	בִּינוֹת	נבונות
קוֹמַ֫מְתִּי	קוֹמַ֫מְתִּי	בַּנְתִּי	בִּינוֹתִי	נבונותי
קוֹמְמוּ	קוֹמְמוּ	בָּ֫נוּ	בִּ֫ינוּ	נָבוֹנוּ
קוֹמַמְתֶּם	קוֹמַמְתֶּם	בַּנְתֶּם	בִּינוֹתֶם	נבונותם
קוֹמַמְתֶּן	קוֹמַמְתֶּן	בַּנְתֶּן	בִּינוֹתֶן	נבונותן
קוֹמַ֫מְנוּ	קוֹמַ֫מְנוּ	בַּ֫נּוּ	בִּינוֹנוּ	נבונ֫וֹנוּ
קוֹמֵם	קוֹמֵם	כִּין	בֵּן	הִבּוֹן
קוֹמֵם		בִּין		הִבּוֹן
קוֹמְמִי		בִּ֫ינִי		etc.
קוֹמְמוּ		בִּ֫ינוּ		
קוֹמֵ֫מְנָה		—		
יְקוֹמֵם	יְקוֹמַם	יָבִין		יִבּוֹן
תְּקוֹמֵם	תְּקוֹמַם	תָּבִין		etc.
תְּקוֹמֵם	תְּקוֹמַם	תָּבִין		
תְּקוֹמְמִי	תְּקוֹמְמִי	תָּבִ֫ינִי		
אֲקוֹמֵם	אֲקוֹמַם	אָבִין		
יְקוֹמְמוּ	יְקוֹמְמוּ	יָבִ֫ינוּ		
תְּקוֹמֵ֫מְנָה	תְּקוֹמַמְנָה	תְּבִינֶ֫ינָה		
תְּקוֹמְמוּ	תְּקוֹמְמוּ	תָּבִ֫ינוּ		
תְּקוֹמֵ֫מְנָה	תְּקוֹמַמְנָה	תְּבִינֶ֫ינָה		
נְקוֹמֵם	נְקוֹמַם	נָבִין		
		יָבֵן		
		וַיָּ֫בֶן		
		יְבִינֵ֫נוּ		
מְקוֹמֵם	מְקוֹמָם	בָּן (בוּן pass.)		נָבִין

עּי. They do not differ from the verbs עּו, except that in this second form the afformatives beginning with a cosonant require also the insertion of a preceding auxiliary וֹ, v g. בַּנֹתֶם, בָּנוּ‏ but בֵּינוֹתָ, בִּינוֹתֶם, בִּינוֹת.

A few of these verbs do not even admit the medial וֹ, as רִיב *he contended*, דִּין *he judged*, שִׂישׂ *he rejoiced*.

§ 42. Verbs ל"א (Lamedh-'Aleph).

The verbs, whose third radical is א, have this peculiarity that the א becomes quiescent whenever the vowel *a* or *e* appears in the last syllable Therefore the Pathach, which otherwise is in the last syllable, is always lengthened into a Kamets Before all the afformatives that begin with a consonant, א quiesces in Tserê in the perfect (except the perf. of Kal med. a, which has a Kamets), and in Seghôl in the future; v g Kal perf sing 3 m. מָצָא, 2 m מָצָאתָ; future sing 3 m יִמְצָא, plur. 2. f תִּמְצֶינָה — Niphal perf. sing 3 m נִמְצָא, 2 m. נִמְצֵאתָ, Hiph perf sing 3. m. הִמְצִיא, 2. m. הִמְצֵאתָ, future sing. 3. m יַמְצִיא, plur 3. f. תַּמְצֶאנָה.

§ 43. Verbs ל"ה (Lamedh-He).

The verbs, whose third radical is ה (whence their name ל"ה), are properly ל"י, and from this twofold character derive the following peculiarities

1 In the formation of the persons, the ה is changed before all additions, thus:

a) in the third pers fem sing of the perf ה is changed into ת: גָּלְתָה for גָּלָה;

b) before all afformatives beginning with a consonant, ה is changed into וֹ, which quiesces in Tserê in the perf. (although Kal and sometimes Piël have Chîrek) and in Seghôl in the imper and the future: תִּגְלֶינָה, נִגְלִיתָ, גָּלִיתָ;

c) before all afformatives beginning with a vowel ה is omitted: תגלי, נְלוּ etc

2. In the formation of the conjugations the following rules are observed:

ה quiesces

in Kamets in all the perfects, גָלָה, נִגְלָה, נְגְלָה etc.

in Tserê in all the imperatives, נָלֵה, הִגְלֵה, גלה etc.

in Seghôl in all the futures and participles, יִגְלֶה, יִגְלֶה, נגְלֶה etc, גלה, יִגְלֶה etc.,

ה is changed into י in the partic. pass נָלוּי,

ה is replaced by the final form וּת in all the infinitives: נְלוֹת, הִגְלוֹת, גלות etc

These verbs have in all their conjugations apocopated imperatives and futures, in which the ה with its Seghôl is omitted, v. g in Niph יִגָל from יִגָלה, in Piël יְגַל from יְגַלה, צַו from צוה   As in this manner Kal and Hiphil acquire forms of three consonants with but one vowel, v g יִגְלֶה, apoc יגל, Hiph יַגְלֶה, apoc יַגל, an auxiliary vowel is placed under the root in order to form a new syllable (§ 18, 1), v g יִגְל future Kal of נְלָה, ישע of שָׂעָה, יַעַשׂ of עָשָׂה.

Note 1   This auxiliary vowel is sometimes omitted, v g וַיִּפֶן, יַרְד, יַפֶת   This occurs especially with the א, because this letter is not supposed to make the syllable end in two consonants, v g וַיַּרְא *he saw.*

2   The Chîrek of the preformative in the apocopated future is frequently lengthened into Tserê, because the syllable is then open (§ 17, 2, *a*), v g ירא, וַיִּפֶן

3   The preformatives of the apocopated imper and future of Hiphil take Seghôl instead of Pathach, unless there be a guttural, v g הַצֵּל, וַיַּתַר, חרב, תֵּרְף, יְגַל

4   The verbs הָיָה *he was* and חָיָה *he lived* have the apocop futures יחי and יחי

5   The three verbs נָאָה *he was beautiful,* שָׂתָה *he darted,* and especially שָׁחָה *he bent down* have, instead of Piel, the form Pilel, and Hithpalel instead of Hithpael, and in these forms they double the last radical, after changing the first ה into ו, v g נַאֲוָה or נָאָוָה *it was becoming,* שַׁחֲוָה *he threw a dart,* הִשְׁתַּחֲוָה, imperf יִשְׁתַּחֲוֶה, apoc. יִשְׁתַּחוּ *he bent down, he worshipped.*

Paradigm of the verb גלֹה;

			Kal.	Niphal.	Piel.
Perf.	*sing.*	3 *m*	נָּלָה	נִגְלָה	גִּלָּה
		3 *f.*	גָּלְתָה	נִגְלְתָה	גִּלְּתָה
		2 *m.*	גָּלִיתָ	נִגְלֵיתָ	גִּלִּיתָ
		2 *f.*	גָּלִית	נגלית	גִּלִּית
		1 *c.*	גָּלִיתִי	נגלֵיתִי	גִּלִּיתִי
	plur.	3 *c.*	גָּלוּ	נגלוּ	גִּלּוּ
		2 *m.*	גליתם	נגלֵיתֶם	גִּלִּיתֶם
		2 *f.*	גליתן	נגליתֶן	גִּלִּיתֶן
		1 *c.*	גָּלִינוּ	נגלֹינוּ	גלֹינוּ
Inf.	*absol.*		גָּלֹה (גָּלוֹ poet	נגלה	גלה
	constr.		גלֹות	הִגָּלוֹה	גַּלּוֹת
Imper.	*sing*	2 *m.*	גלה	הִגָּלֵה	גַּלֵה
		2 *f.*	גלי	הִגָּלִי	גַּלִּי
	plur.	2 *m*	גלוּ	הִגָּלוּ	גַּלּוּ
		2 *f.*	גלֶֹינָה	הִגָּלֶֹינָה	גַּלֶֹּינָה
Fut	*sing.*	3 *m.*	יגלה	יִגָּלֶה	יְגַלֶּה
		3 *f.*	תגלה	תִּגָּלֶה	תְּגַלֶּה
		2 *m.*	תגלה	תִּגָּלֶה	תְּגַלֶּה
		2 *f.*	תגלי	תִּגָּלִי	תְּגַלִּי
		1 *c.*	אגלה	אֶגָּלֶה	אֲגַלֶּה
	plur.	3 *m.*	יגלו	יִגָּלוּ	יְגַלּוּ
		3 *f.*	תגלֶֹינָה	תִּגָּלֶֹינָה	תְּגַלֶֹּינָה
		2 *m.*	תגלו	תִּגָּלוּ	תְּגַלּוּ
		2 *f.*	תגלֶֹינָה	תִּגָּלֶֹינָה	תְּגַלֶֹּינָה
		1 *c.*	נגלה	נִגָּלֶה	נְגַלֶּה
Fut.	*apoc.*		יִגֶל	יִגָּל	יְגַל
Fut.	*with suffix.*		יגלני		יְגַלֵּנִי
Part.	*act.*		גֹּלֶה	נִגְלֶה	מְגַלֶּה
	pass.		גָּלוּי		

גָּלָה *he revealed.*

Pual.	Hiphil	Hophal	Hithpael
גֻּלָּה	הִגְלָה	הָגְלָה	הִתְגַּלָּה
גֻּלְּתָה	הִגְלְתָה	הָגְלְתָה	הִתְגַּלְּתָה
גֻּלֵּיתָ	הִגְלֵיתָ	הָגְלֵיתָ	הִתְגַּלֵּיתָ
גֻּלֵּית	הִגְלֵית	הָגְלֵית	הִתְגַּלֵּית
גֻּלֵּיתִי	הִגְלֵיתִי	הָגְלֵיתִי	הִתְגַּלֵּיתִי
גֻּלּוּ	הִגְלוּ	הָגְלוּ	הִתְגַּלּוּ
גֻּלֵּיתֶם	הִגְלֵיתֶם	הָגְלֵיתֶם	הִתְגַּלֵּיתֶם
גֻּלֵּיתֶן	הִגְלֵיתֶן	הָגְלֵיתֶן	הִתְגַּלֵּיתֶן
גֻּלֵּינוּ	הִגְלֵינוּ	הָגְלֵינוּ	הִתְגַּלֵּינוּ
גֻּלֹּה	הַגְלֵה	הָגְלֵה	הִתְגַּלֵּה
גֻּלּוֹת	הַגְלוֹת	הָגְלוֹת	הִתְגַּלּוֹת
	הַגְלֵה		הִתְגַּלֵּה
	הַגְלִי		הִתְגַּלִּי
	הַגְלוּ		הִתְגַּלּוּ
	הַגְלֶינָה		הִתְגַּלֶּינָה
יְגֻלֶּה	יַגְלֶה	יָגְלֶה	יִתְגַּלֶּה
תְּגֻלֶּה	תַּגְלֶה	תָּגְלֶה	תִּתְגַּלֶּה
תְּגֻלֶּה	תַּגְלֶה	תָּגְלֶה	תִּתְגַּלֶּה
תְּגֻלִּי	תַּגְלִי	תָּגְלִי	תִּתְגַּלִּי
אֲגֻלֶּה	אַגְלֶה	אָגְלה	אֶתְגַּלֶּה
יְגֻלּוּ	יַגְלוּ	יָגְלוּ	יִתְגַּלּוּ
תְּגֻלֶּינָה	תַּגְלֶינָה	תָּגְלֶינָה	תִּתְגַּלֶּינָה
תְּגֻלּוּ	תַּגְלוּ	תָּגְלוּ	תִּתְגַּלּוּ
תְּגֻלֶּינָה	תַּגְלֶינָה	תָּגְלֶינָה	תִּתְגַּלֶּינָה
נְגֻלֶּה	נַגְלֶה	נָגְלֶה	נִתְגַּלֶּה
	יֶגֶל		יִתְגַּל
	יַגְלֵנִי		
מְגֻלֶּה	מַגְלֶה	מָגְלֶה	מִתְגַּלֶּה

4*

§ 44. General remarks on the irregular verbs.

1 Some verbs on account of the nature of their radicals have at the same time a twofold or even a threefold irregularity; v g the verb נָכָה is Pê-Nûn and also Lamedh-He, which sometimes causes that of the whole root only the כ remains: future Hiph יַכֶּה, apoc וַיַּךְ.

2 There are irregular verbs, especially monosyllabic ones, which vary in their inflections so as to be conjugated according to two different paradigms, and this either with one only or with two different significations, v g. נוד, נָדַד, נָדָה *he fled*, פוּר *he broke*, פָּרָה and פָּרָא *he brought forth* (peperit), פָּרַר *he split*

3 There are verbs, of which only some forms are used *(defective verbs)*, and this generally in such a manner that the forms which are wanting are supplemented by those which are borrowed from another root, v g טוֹב *it was good*, future ייטב (from the root יָטַב); יָגֹר *he feared*, future יָגוּר (from גור), הָלַךְ *he went*, future ילך (from יָלַךְ)

§ 45. How to distinguish one monosyllabic root from another.

When, after the elimination of afformatives and preformatives, there remains a root with two consonants, the verb is seen to be either פֶּן or פִּי, or עֵע, or עוּ, or עִי, or לה

1 It will be a פֶּן if the first consonant has a Daghesh-forte (see, however, § 7, note 2 about shevated letters omitting the Daghesh) To find, therefore, the root in the vocabulary, a נ should be placed before the two radicals. Should the word not be found under the letter נ, it must be looked for under י, for it may belong to the class of the verbs פִּי which follow the rules of פֶּן

2 The verbs פִּי show a monosyllable, in the infin, imper. and future of Kal and Hiphil, which forms can easily be known by their punctuation The infin ends in

ה— The only care to be taken is not to confound them with the verbs פֿ

3. The עֹ verbs can be easily mistaken for פֿי and פֿן verbs, but this only in the imper and future. Their difference consists in having a Chôlem as vowel and a Kamets under the preformative   They might also be confounded with the עֹו; but the Daghesh-forte and the punctuation easily distinguish them, since the Shûrek and the Chôlem belong exclusively to the verbs עֹו

4 The verbs עֹו and עֹי can be confounded only with the עֹע, about which see § 40

5 The verbs לֹה can cause a doubt only in the apocopated future   Here however, they are known by the vowel of their preformative, which is a Chîrek parvum (Tserê) or a Pathach in an open syllable

---

B. The pronoun.

§ 46. The demonstrative pronoun.

The demonstrative pronoun has these principal forms:

Sing
{
masc זֶה *this, that,*
fem זֹאת (זֹה, זֹו) *this, that,*
(com זֹו in poetry, and הַלָּז *this, that*)
}

Plur comm אֵלֶּה (אֵל) *these, those*

Besides the forms enclosed in brackets, which are rare, there are still rare forms: masc. לָזֶה, הַלָּזֶה, fem הַלֵּזוּ, all sing

Note. Regarding the use of the article, as a demonstrative pronoun, see § 51.

⨯ § 47. The relative pronoun.

This is especially the particle אֲשֶׁר, which remains the same in every number and gender   Sometimes it is replaced by שַׁ with a Daghesh following (less often שֶׁ or שׁ), which is attached to a word as its prefix, v g. שֶׁלֹּא *who not*

Paradigm of the personal

Nominative of pronoun,	Accusative of pronoun,
separate pronoun.	

A.

ordinary forms:

Sing. 1. *comm* אָנֹכִי,

אֲנִי, in a pause אָנִי, *I.*

נִי ; נִי‍ֽ‍ ; נִי‍ֽ‍— *me*

2   m. (אַתָּ) אַתָּה,

    in pause אָתָּה   } *thou*

  f   אַתְּ (אַתִּי)

הָ —, in pause הָ‍ֽ‍ ‍, ‍ךָ‍ֽ‍ ;

ךָ —, ‍ךָ‍ֽ‍ , ‍ךְ ; ‍ךְ } *thee.*

3.   m. הוּא *he*

    f. הִיא *she.*

הוּ‍—, ‍ו (ה)‍ֽ‍, ‍ו ; הוֹ‍ֽ‍—, הוֹ *him*

הָ ; הָ‍ֽ‍—ָה ; ‍ָה‍ֽ‍‍ *her.*

Plur. 1 *comm.* אֲנַחְנוּ

(אָנוּ, נַחְנוּ) *we.*

נוּ ; נוּ‍ֽ‍ ; נוּ‍ֽ‍— *us*

2   m. אַתֶּם

    f. אַתֵּן, אַתֵּנָה } *you.*

כֶם—

כֶן— } *you (accus.).*

3   m. הֵמָּה, הֵם *they*

, ם‍ֽ‍—, הֶם ; הֶם, ם

‍ֽ‍— מוֹ , ם‍ֽ‍—, ם—, מוֹ‍ֽ‍ *them.*

    f. הֵן, הֵנָּה *they.*

ן, הֵן ; ן‍ֽ‍—, ן‍ֽ‍— ; ן‍ֽ‍— *them.*

---

*) The forms with a star are poetical, and those in brackets are rare.

and possessive pronouns.

suffix of verb	*Genitive of pronoun,* suffix of noun (possessive pronoun).	
B. with Nûn epentheticum.	**A.** of the singular noun	**B.** of the plural noun
פַּֽ־ֶ֫־, פָּֽ־ֶ֫	־ִי mine, my.	־ַי mine, my.
הָ־	הָ—, in Pause ⎫ thine, thy. הָ־ ⎬ ־ְךָ, ד ⎭	יךָ־ ⎫ thine, thy. ־ַ֫יִךְ ⎬ ⎭
נוּ־ֶ֫, כֶּ־	הוּ־, ־ו; הוּ־ֹ, ־ו (ה) his.	־יהוּ ⎫ ־ָיו, ־ָיו his.
פֶּֽ־ָ֫ה	הָ, ־ָה; ⎫ her. ־ֶ֫הָ ⎬ ⎭	־ֶ֫יהָ her.
פֻּֽ־ֵ֫נוּ	נוּ־ֹ; נוּ־ our.	־ֵ֫ינוּ our.
	־כֶם ⎫ your. ־כֶן ⎬ ⎭	־יכֶם ⎫ your. ־יכֶן ⎬ ⎭
	־ָם; ־הֶם ⎫ ־ָ֫מוֹ ⎬ their. ־ָן, הֶן, הֵן ⎭	־יהֶם ⎫ ־ֵ֫ימוֹ ⎬ their. ־יהֶן ⎭

⨯ **§ 48. The interrogative pronoun.**

There are two interrogative pronouns מִי, *who?* said of persons, and מָה (fem), *what?* said of things only This second form is generally joined to the next word by a Makkeph and then it has, except before א and ר, the form מַה־ with the Daghesh-forte conjunctive, v g מַה־יָּעֲשֶׂה, מַה־זֹּאת, מַה־אֵלֶּה; it is even united into one word with it, v. g מַלָּכֶם *quid vobis?* (§ 16, c)

This pronoun מָה becomes מֶה before words that begin with הָ, חָ or עָ, v g מֶה עָשִׂיתָ *what hast thou done?*

§ 49. The personal and the possessive pronouns.

The personal pronoun is either a selfsubsisting word (separate pronoun), or an addition only to the verb or to the noun, or even to particles (suffix pronoun) The separate pronoun indicates the nominative; the suffix of the noun indicates the genitive of the pronoun, or what is the same, the possessive pronoun; the suffix of the verb indicates the object of the verb or the accusative

Note 1   The suffixes and afformatives are primitive forms of the pronouns The separate pronoun of the 1 and 2. person is clearly composed of the ancient noun אָן and the suffixes, so that אָנֹכִי is the same as *my person*, אָתֶם (for אָן תֶם) *your person,* etc.

2   It will help the memory to notice a) that only in the 1 person the suffix of the noun is somewhat different from the suffix of the verb, and b) that the suffixes of plural nouns differ from those in the singular in their having a Yôdh before them

§ 50. The Verb with suffixes.

1   The suffixes of the verb (with the exception of ה, כֶם and כֶן) are of a threefold form: 1 the simple form, which begins with a consonant, and is added to the forms of the verb that end in a vowel, v g קְטָלוּנִי–נִי; 2 with the *agglutination point A*; this suffix is added to the forms of the perfect that end in a consonant, v. g קְטָלַנִי–ַנִי;

3. with the *agglutination point E*; this suffix is added to
those forms of the imper and future which end in a consonant, as נִי— – יִקְטְלֵנִי.

2 Besides the ordinary forms of suffixes there are also
sometimes others used which are called suffixes with the
epenthetic Nûn; they are found in the third column (in
regard to them see § 13, note about assimilation of ה with
preceding נ)

3. The forms of the verb undergo considerable changes
when they receive suffixes, especially on account of the
moving of the accent

a Perfect
Kal

Sing		Plur.	
3 masc	קְטָל, קְטָלֽ	3. comm	קְטָלוּ
3 fem	קְטָלַת		
2 masc	(קְטַלְתּ) קְטַלְתְּ	2. comm	קְטַלְתּוּ
2 fem	קְטַלְתִּי		
1 comm	קְטַלְתִּי	1 comm	קְטַלְנוּ

Thus the first vowel is omitted everywhere because it
no longer precedes the accent (§ 18, 3)

In the perfect of Piël, the Tserê of the root before ה,
כֶם and כֶן is changed into Seghôl; before the other suffixes
it is entirely thrown out

Hiphil remains unchanged

The three other conjugations, being passive or reflexive,
do not take suffixes

b Future

The Chôlem of the future of Kal before ה, כֶם and כֶן
is changed into Kamets-chatûph; v g יִקְטֹל - יִקְטָלְךָ *(yiktŏl°cha)*;
it is entirely omitted before the other suffixes.

The verbs which have *A* in the imperf retain the same,
but change the Pathach into Kamets when the syllable becomes an open one

Paradigm of the regular

		1 Sing. comm me.	2 Sing m thee.	2 Sing f thee.	3. Sing. m him.
He killed					
Perf. Kal. sing. 3 m.		קְטָלַ֫נִי	קְטָלְךָ	קְטָלֵךְ	קְטָלָ֫הוּ קְטָלוֹ
	3 f.	קְטָלַ֫תְנִי	קְטָלַ֫תֶךָ	קְטָלָ֫תֶךְ	קְטָלַ֫תְהוּ קְטָלַ֫תּוּ
	2 m	קְטַלְתַּ֫נִי קְטַלְתָּ֫נִי } [1]	—	—	קְטַלְתָּ֫הוּ קְטַלְתּוֹ
	2 f.	קְטַלְתִּ֫ינִי	—	—	קְטַלְתִּ֫יהוּ קְטַלְתִּיו
	1 c.	—	קְטַלְתִּ֫יךָ	קְטַלְתִּיךְ	קְטַלְתִּיו
	plur. 3 c.	קְטָל֫וּנִי	קְטָל֫וּךָ	קְטָל֫וּךְ	קְטָל֫וּהוּ
	2 m.	קְטַלְתּ֫וּנִי	—	—	קְטַלְתּ֫וּהוּ
	1 c.	—	קְטַלְנ֫וּךָ	קְטַלְנ֫וּךְ	קְטַלְנ֫וּהוּ
Inf. Kal. suff. of noun. suff. of verb.		קָטְלִי קָטְלֵ֫נִי }	קָטְלֶךָ קָטְלֶךָ }	קָטְלֵךְ	קָטְלוֹ
Imper. Kal.		קָטְלֵ֫נִי	—	—	קָטְל֫וֹהוּ
Fut. Kal. sing. 3 m.		יִקְטְלֵ֫נִי	יִקְטָלְךָ	יקטלך	יִקְטְלֵ֫הוּ
3 m. with Nûn epenth.		יִקְטְלֵ֫נִּי	יִקְטְלֶ֫ךָּ	—	יִקְטְלֶ֫נּוּ
plur. 3 m.		יִקְטְל֫וּנִי	יִקְטְל֫וּךָ	יקטלוך	יִקְטְל֫וּהוּ
Perf. Piël.		קִטְּלַ֫נִי	קִטְּלְךָ	קִטְּלֵךְ	קִטְּלוֹ

verb with suffixes.

3 Sing. f · her.	1 Plur comm · us	2 Plur m · you	2 Plur. f · you.	3 Plur. m · them.	3 Plur f · them
קְטָלָהּ	קְטָלָנוּ	קְטַלְכֶם	קְטַלְכֶן	קְטָלָם	קְטָלָן
קְטָלַתָּה	קְטָלַתְנוּ	קְטָלַתְכֶם	קְטָלַתְכֶן	קְטָלָתַם	קְטָלָתַן
קְטַלְתָּהּ	קַטַלְתָּנוּ	—	—	קְטַלְתָּם	קְטַלְתָן
קְטַלְתִּיהָ	קְטַלְתִּינוּ	—	—	קְטַלְתִּים	קְטַלְתִּין
קְטַלְתִּיהָ	—	קְטַלְתִּיכֶם	קְטַלְתִּיכן	קְטַלְתִּים	קְטַלְתִּין
קְטָלוֹהָ	קְטָלוֹנוּ	קְטָלוֹכֶם	קְטָלוּכֶן	קְטָלוֹם	קְטָלוּן
קְטַלְתּוֹהָ	קְטַלְתּוֹנוּ	—	—	קְטַלְתּוּם	קְטַלְתּוּן
קְטַלְנוֹהָ	—	קְטַלְנוּכם	קְטַלְנוּכן	קְטַלְנוּם	קְטַלְנוּן
קָטְלָהּ	קָטְלֵנוּ	קָטְלְכֶם	קָטְלְכֶן	קָטְלָם	קָטְלָן
קָטְלָהָ / קָטְלָהּ	קָטְלֵנוּ	—	—	קָטְלם	—
יְקְטֹלָהָ / יִקְטְלָהּ	יִקְטְלֶנּוּ	יִקְטָלְכֶם	יִקְטָלְכֶן	יִקְטְלֵם	יִקְטְלֵן
יקטְלֶנָה	יִקְטְלֶנּוּ	—	—	—	—
יִקְטְלוֹהָ	יקטלוֹנוּ	יקטלוכם	יקטלוכן	יקטלום	יִקְטְלוּן
קַטְּלָהּ	קַטְּלָנוּ	קַטְּלכֶם	קַטְּלכֶן	קַטְּלָם	קַטְּלָן

In Piël the Tserê is thrown out or shortened, as above
Hiphil does not change

Instead of the feminine form of the 2 and 3 pers.
plur in נָה, the masc form ו is used, v. g. תִּקְטְלוּנִי *you
(women) will kill me*

<h3 style="text-align:center">c Infinitive</h3>

The infinitive of Kal when receiving suffixes appears
in the form קְטֹל *(kŏtᵉl)*, and according to its power takes
either the suffix of the verb or that of the noun; thus
v g. קָטְלֵנִי *(kŏtᵉlenî)* with the suffix of the verb, that is
the accusative, means *my being killed*, whereas קָטְלִי *(kŏtᵉlî)*
with the suffix of the noun, that is the possessive pronoun,
signifies *my killing (somebody)*

<h3 style="text-align:center">d Imperative</h3>

The form of the imperative with suffixes is the same
as that of the infinitive, viz קְטֹל   The forms קְטְלִי and
קִטְלוּ remain, and the latter serves also for the feminine

<h3 style="text-align:center">e Participle</h3>

The participles of Kal and Piël lose Tserê, and like the
infinitive take the suffixes either of the verb or of the noun.

Note   The verbs לֹּה lose ה with its vowel before all suffixes,
v g עָנֵּנִי from עָנָה, צוּךְ *(tsivvᵉcha)* from צִוָּה Piel of צָוָה

C. The Noun.

× § 51. The article.

The primitive form of the article was הַל   Afterwards,
however, the article ceased to be a separate word, and became a prefix of the noun; its ל is assimilated with the
first consonant of the word according to rules of §§ 11
and 13. In this way three forms arise:

1 (·)הַ, that is, *He* with Pathach and following Daghesh-
forte, either written or implicit, and this is the common

form, v g הַדָּבָר *the word*, הַסּוּס *the horse*, הַחֹדֶשׁ *the month*, הַחָכְמָה (*hachŏchmâ*) *the wisdom.*

2 הָ, *He* with Kamets This form is always used before א and ר and ordinarily before ע and ה (see 3), v. g הָאִישׁ *the man*, הָראֹשׁ *the head*, הָעֶבֶד *the servant*, הָהַר *the mountain*

3 הֶ, *He* with Seghôl and no Daghesh This form is used especially before ה, ח and ע when they have not the accent, or when they have Kamets for vowel, v g הֶהָרִים *the mountains*, הֶחָזוֹן *the vision*, הֶעָרִים *the cities*

The article is placed not only before substantives, but also before adjectives and pronouns, v g הַהוּא (*the*) *that* one, הָהֵמָה *the same.*

§ 52. Substantive and adjective nouns.

Substantives and adjectives in Hebrew do not in their form differ from each other. Nor have the adjectives a special form for the comparative or superlative degrees Adverbs likewise do not differ in form from substantives

The noun is either of the masculine or of the feminine gender; there is no neuter in Hebrew The masculine gender has no termination of its own; the feminine ends ordinarily in ה-ָ and ת—, more rarely in ת-ָ, ת-ֶ, ית—, ר, ות; it sometimes even has no special termination

There are three numbers in Hebrew: the singular, the plural, and the dual The last is used for objects that are twofold by nature, as the eyes, the hands, etc

As to the formation of nouns, they are: a) primitive, expressing the simplest ideas as עיר *city* or b) derivative, and these in turn are α) denominative, derived from a noun, as קַשָּׁת *archer*, from קֶשֶׁת *bow* and β) verbal, derived from a verb. These are *nomina nuda* if they have like the verb three consonants and two vowels as עבד *a servant*, from עָבַד *he labored;* they are *augmented nouns* if the root

has been increased by means of letters added to it, before
or after, as מִשְׁפָּט *judgment*, from שָׁפַט *he judged*. This
augment of nouns is effected by any of the seven servile
or he'emantic letters א, ה, ו, י, מ, נ, ת (הָאֵמַנְתִּיו).

§ 53. Declension of nouns.

There is properly speaking no declension of nouns in the Semitic
languages, what we call here by that name is such by analogy only
for the sake of comparison with European tongues

1 The dative is formed by means of the preposition
לְ, the ablative by prefixing בְ (*by*), or מִן (*from, by*)

· When the noun has both the article and the letters
לְ or בְ as prefixes, the ה of the article is omitted and its
vowel is written under the preposition, v g דָּבָר *word*,
dat. לְדָבָר, but הַדָּבָר *the word*, dat לַדָּבָר *to the word;*
הֶעָלֹז *the violence*, בֶּעָלֹז *by the violence*.

The preposition מִן leaves the article unchanged, and is
written either separately or in combination with the following
word according to § 16 and 11, v. g. מִן הָאָרֶץ, מִן הַשָּׁמַיִם,
מֵהָאִישׁ, מִשָּׁמֶשׁ

2. The accusative is expressed either by the simple
form of the noun, or, when the noun is in any manner
understood as definite, by prefixing the particle אֵת or
אֶת־, v. g. אֶת־הַדָּבָר or אֵת הַדָּבָר *the word* or *the thing,*
אֵת בְּנוֹ, אֶת־דָּוִיד, אֶת־הָאִישׁ *his son*

Note. The primitive termination of the accusative was ־ָה
(local *He*), which still is used to denote local motion towards some
place or thing, and leaves the accent unchanged, v g הַבַּיְתָה *towards
the house* or *into the house* (from בַּיִת), אַרְצָה *into the land* or *towards
the earth* from אֶרֶץ (or אָרֶץ), בָּבֶלָה *to Babylon.*

✗ § 54. The construct state (genitive).

The Hebrews use a peculiar construction to signify
that one noun depends on another They put the governing
noun in what is called the construct state, by means of
which it becomes, so to speak, one word with the depending

noun, as דְּבַר יְהוָה *the word of the Lord,* כָּל־הָעָם *the totality of the people,* יַם־מֶלַח *the sea of salt.* Thus a form with shorter vowels arises, which is called the construct state, whereas the form of a noun, on which no other depends, is the absolute state Yet there are words which do not undergo any change in the construct state, v g. סוּס, *a horse,* סוּס־הַמֶּלֶךְ *the horse of the king,* מֶלֶךְ יִשְׂרָאֵל *the king of Israel.* Most nouns change not only when they are in the construct state, but also when they are in the plural or when they receive suffixes Of these mention will be made presently; we now give a paradigm of nouns with suffixes, that remain unchanged See p 64.

✗ § 55. How nouns are changed in the formation of the construct state, in the masculine and feminine singular.

1. Construct state of masc sing To form the construct state of any form of noun no vowels are changed but the Kamets and the Tserê, both of which, with the exception of segolate nouns (see below), in the masc. sing. become Pathach in the last syllable, and Sheʿvâ in the penult, v g דָּבָר, constr state דְּבַר, זָקֵן, constr. state זְקַן. Gutturals of course instead of a simple Sheʿvâ take a Chateph, v. g חָצֵר *a villa,* construct state חֲצַר, עָנָף *a branch,* constr. state עֲנַף

2 Construct state of femin sing The feminine form ־ָה is changed into ־ַת in the construct state, v g מַלְכַת מִצְרַיִם *the queen of Egypt,* and if the penult has a Kamets or a Tserê, they are changed into a Sheʿvâ, as said above, v. g. עֵצָה *counsel* — עֲצַת The feminine terminations ־ֶת, ־ִית, ות remain unchanged in the construct state, v. g. מַלְכוּת כַּשְׂדִּים *the reign of the Chaldeans.*

✗ § 56. Plural of masculine nouns.

The plural of masculine nouns is formed by the termination ־ִים (rarely ־ִין), added to the construct state of

Suffixes of sing.

masc

		sing		plur	
1	c.	סוּסִי my horse		סוּסֵנוּ our horse	
2	m.	סוּסְךָ thy h		סוּסְכֶם your h.	
	f.	סוּסֵךְ thy h		סוּסְכֶן your h	
3	m.	סוּסוֹ his h		סוּסָם their h	
	f.	סוּסָהּ her h		סוּסָן their h.	

fem

		sing		plur	
1	c.	סוּסָתִי my mare		סוּסָתֵנוּ our mare	
2.	m.	סוּסָתְךָ thy m		סוּסַתְכֶם your m	
	f.	סוּסָתֵךְ thy m		סוּסַתְכֶן your m	
3.	m	סוּסָתוֹ his m		סוּסָתָם their m	
	f.	סוּסָתָהּ her m		סוּסָתָן their m	

Suffixes of plur.

masc

		sing		plur	
1.	c.	סוּסַי my horses		סוּסֵינוּ our horses	
2	m	סוּסֶיךָ thy h		סוּסֵיכֶם your h	
	f.	סוּסַיִךְ thy h		סוּסֵיכֶן your h	
3.	m	סוּסָיו his h.		סוּסֵיהֶם their h	
	f	סוּסֶיהָ her h		סוּסֵיהֶן their h	

fem

		sing		plur	
1	c.	סוּסוֹתַי my mares		סוּסוֹתֵינוּ our mares	
2.	m.	סוּסוֹתֶיךָ thy m.		סוּסוֹתֵיכֶם your m	
	f.	סוּסוֹתַיִךְ thy m		סוּסוֹתֵיכֶן your m	
3	m.	סוּסוֹתָיו his m		סוּסוֹתֵיהֶם their m.	
	f.	סוּסוֹתֶיהָ her m		סוּסוֹתֵיהֶן their m.	

the singular, v. g פָּקִיד–פָּקִיד–פְּקִידִים. But if the vowel of the last syllable were shortened on account of the construct state (§ 55), it is again lengthened either into Kamets or into Tserê, according to § 17, 2 *a* v. g דָּבָר, constr state דְּבַר, plur. דְּבָרִים; זָקֵן *old man*, constr state זְקַן, plur זְקֵנִים.

§ 57. The dual.

The dual is similarly formed by adding to the construct state of the singular the termination ־ַיִם, v. g. דְּבַר, dual דְּבָרַיִם

× § 58. Construct state of the plural and dual.

The form of the construct state is the same for the plural and the dual It is formed by changing the plural and dual termination ־ִים and ־ַיִם into ־ֵי, and also changing Tserê and Kamets in the manner described for the masc sing (§ 55), v g בֵּן *son*, plur בָּנִים, constr. state בְּנֵי Should it happen that — the first vowel having been elided already on account of the plural, and now the penult losing also its vowel — there should be two vowelless consonants, the first receives an auxiliary vowel (§ 18), v g דָּבָר, plur דְּבָרִים, constr state of plur. דִּבְרֵי; חָצֵר, plur. חֲצֵרִים, constr state חַצְרֵי

§ 59. Plural and dual of feminine nouns.

1 The plural of feminine nouns is formed by changing the termination ־ָה into וֹת, v g. שָׁנָה *year*, plur. שָׁנוֹת; the same is done for the other feminine terminations ־ֶת or ־ַת, etc , v. g. מַאֲכֶלֶת *knife*, plur מַאֲכָלוֹת. Should the singular noun have no proper feminine termination, וֹת is simply added, v g. כַּף *palm of the hand*, plur כַּפּוֹת

2. The construct state of the plural retains the termination וֹת, but Kamets and Tserê are thrown out in the penult, v. g. שָׁנוֹת, constr. state שְׁנוֹת.

3 The dual of feminine nouns is formed from the construct state of the singular by means of the changes indicated in § 56, and by adding the termination ־ַיִם, v. g. שָׂפָה *lip*, שְׂפָתַיִם *the two lips* The construct state is derived from this form in the same way as the masculines from their dual (§ 58), v g. שִׂפְתֵי.

4. If a noun has besides the termination ־ָה also one in ־ַת, the former serves to make the plural, the latter to make the construct state of the singular, v. g. דְּבַר, fem. דִּבְרָה and דְּבָרַת, constr. state דְּבָרַת, plur דְּברות; מַמְלָכָה *reign*, constr state מַמְלֶכֶת, plur. מַמְלָכוֹת

Note. Some feminine nouns have in the plural the masculine termination ־ים, and masculines vice versa the termination ות These irregularities are noted in the dictionary

§ 60. Addition of suffixes.

1. Nouns in the singular take suffixes different from those in the plural. The suffixes of plural nouns are characterized by a preceding Yôdh (except the 1. pers sing. ־ַי where the characteristic of the plural is the Pathach, v. g. דְּבָרִי *my word*, דְּבָרַי *my words*).

There are, moreover, light and grave suffixes. The grave suffixes are those which per se make a closed syllable, viz. כֶם, כֶן, הֶם and הֶן. Their influence differs from the others in this that they do not draw to themselves the last consonant of the root, so that the last syllable before a grave suffix does not undergo any change in its vowel, v g דְּבָרְךָ *thy word*, דְּבַרְכֶם *your word*.

2 The following is the rule for affixing suffixes to the regular noun (as distinct from Segolates).

The suffixes, both light and grave, of the singular, and the light suffixes of the plural masc. require their noun to be in the construct state of the singular, v. g. דְּבָרִיךָ, דְּבַרְכֶם, דְּבָרִי; but the grave suffixes of the plural, as also the light suffixes of the plural femin , are joined to the construct state of the plural, v. g. דִּבְרֵיכֶם *your words*, שְׁנוֹתַי *my years*.

In all these cases remember the rule given § 17, 2 a. Paradigms will be given synoptically below, I and II.

§ 61. Segolate nouns.

1 There is a class of triliteral nouns, which are derived immediately from the root, and are characterized by having Seghôl in the last syllable and the accent on the first. Originally these nouns were monosyllables, ending in two consonants, as קְטֹל, קְטֹל, קְטֹל; they, however, according to § 18, 1 took an auxiliary vowel, which made the first syllable an open one and gave to these segolate nouns the forms of קֹטֶל, קֳטָל, קֶטֶל, or with the concurrence of a guttural פֶּעַל, פֹּעַל, פַּעַל, the accent being everywhere on the first syllable

Should there be a double consonant in the root, no auxiliary vowel is assumed, but the two consonants are assimilated, and the vowel lengthened, v g יָם for יַמם, אֵם for אֵמם, חֹק for חֳקק.

2 This auxiliary Seghôl is omitted, and the original punctuation with one vowel in the root is brought back, as soon as there is any addition to the end of the word, v. g מֶלֶךְ *king*, מַלְכִּי *my king* Thus the ancient form is used with most suffixes (See except. § 63)

Note The primitive monosyllabic form is found sometimes with a long vowel in the absolute state: גֵּיא *a valley*, חֵטְא *a sin*, קֹשְׁט *the truth*, שָׁוְא *vanity*

§ 62. Plural of the segolates.

All segolate forms have Sh⁼vâ and Kamets in the plural, v g. מֶלֶךְ, plur מְלָכִים; סֵפֶר, plur. סְפָרִים Those whose root is *o*, generally take the Chateph-Kamets, even under non-guttural letters, v g. קֳדָשִׁים (קָדְשִׁים — *kŏdhashîm*)

The construct state of the plural is derived from the primitive form: קָדְשֵׁי, סִפְרֵי, מַלְכֵי (*kŏdh⁼shê*).

5*

§ 63. Suffixes of the segolates.

The plural form with Shᵉvâ and Kamets serves also for the light suffix of the plural, v. g. סְפָרַי *my books.* All the other suffixes are added to the ancient form, v. g סִפְרִי *my book,* קָדְשְׁכֶם (*kodhshᵉchem*) *your holiness,* גָּדְלוֹ *his greatness*

Paradigm of ordinary segolates, below N. III.

§ 64. Segolates with gutturals.

If the second or third consonant of a segolate is a guttural, it is not Seghôl, but Pathach, that is assumed as auxiliary, and if *a* is the radical vowel, that sound also remains Pathach, v g נַעַר, נֶצַח   Other forms are not affected by this rule

See paradigm below, N IV.

§ 65. Segolates derived from roots לָ"ה

The segolate nouns that are formed from roots לָ"ה, have their ה sometimes changed into י with Chîrek as auxiliary vowel v. g פְּרִי *fruit,* which noun is derived from the ancient form פֶּרִי (from פָּרָה *he was fertile*), חֳלִי *sickness,* but also בְּכֶה *a weeping,* רֵעֶה *a friend,* חֹזֶה *a seer.*

§ 66. Segolates from roots עָ"וּ and עָ"י.

In segolate nouns derived from roots עָ"וּ and עָ"י, the middle radical is a true consonant   They, therefore, deviate from the usual formation and treatment of segolates only inasmuch as they follow the rules which concern the semivowels, v. g מָוֶת for מָוֶת (§ 17, 2 *a*), בַּיִת for בַּיִת (§ 18, 1), שׁוֹט *a scourge* for שׁוֹט, רוּחַ *spirit* for רְוּחַ (§ 12, 2)   As seen in the paradigm the semivowel in the construct state coalesces everywhere with the vowel. The plural is formed either from the construct state of the singular or according to the rule of § 62, v. g זֵיתִים *olives* from זַיִת, עֵינוֹת and עֲיָנוֹת *fountains* from עַיִן, תְּיָשִׁים *buckgoats* from תַּיִשׁ, שְׁוָקִים *routes* from שׁוּק

See paradigm below, N VI

§ 67. Feminine segolates.

1 Feminine nouns are often formed from masculine segolates by terminating them in ה—ָ, v. g מֶלֶךְ *king*, מַלְכָה *queen*. These feminine nouns are declined in the same way as the regular ones (N II); but in the plural, like all segolates, they have Shevâ and Kamets, v. g מְלָכוֹת *queens*, יְלָדוֹת *girls*

2 The feminine termination ת— makes forms whose ending is *per se* of a segolate nature, whence in the singular they are entirely treated as segolates, v g אִגֶּרֶת *epistle*, אִגַּרְתְּכֶם, אִגַּרְתִּי   The plural is differently formed as shown in the paradigm

See paradigm below, N IX

§ 68. Monosyllabic nouns derived from roots עּע.

Nouns derived from roots עּע are monosyllables (see § 61), v. g עַז, אֵם, רָם. Whenever they receive an afformative augment, they take a Daghesh-forte in the final consonant, and shorten their vowel, v g (שֵׁן) שִׁנַּיִם, אִמּוֹת, רַמִּי *teeth*, חֻקָּיו *his precepts* from חֹק

Note   To these should be added a) a few nouns which by assimilating a medial Nûn became monosyllables, as אַף *anger* for אַנְף, whence אַפִּי; b) some triliteral nouns in which the final consonant is doubled, v g גָּמָל *a camel*, plur. גְּמַלִּים

§ 69. Index of irregular nouns.

1. אָב *father*; constr. st אֲבִי, plur. אָבוֹת; with light suff. אָבִי, with grave suff. אֲבִי, v g אֲבִיךָ, אָבִיךָ, אֲבִיכֶם

2. אָח *brother*; constr. st אֲחִי, plur. אַחִים; with light suff. אָחִי, with grave אֲחִי, suff of plur of 1. pers sing. אַחַי, 3 pers אֶחָיו.

3 אָחוֹת *sister*; plur. אֲחָיוֹת; with suff. אַחְיוֹתָיו or אֲחוֹתֵךְ.

4. אִישׁ *man*; has the plural of the noun אֱנָשִׁים (אֱנוֹשׁ

I

Masculines with Kamets and Tserê.

Sing. absol.	דָּבָר	חָכָם	זָקֵן	חָצֵר
— constr.	דְּבַר	חֲכַם	זְקַן	חֲצַר
— with light suff.	דְּבָרִי	חֲכָמִי	זְקֵנִי	חֲצֵרִי
— with grave suff.	דְּבַרְכֶם	חֲכַמְכֶם	זְקַנְכֶם	חֲצַרְכֶם
Plur absol	דְּבָרִים	חֲכָמִים	זְקֵנִים	חֲצֵרִים
— (and dual) constr.	דִּבְרֵי	חַכְמֵי	זִקְנֵי	חַצְרֵי
— with light suff.	דְּבָרַי	חֲכָמַי	זְקֵנַי	חֲצֵרַי
— with grave suff.	דִּבְרֵיכֶם	חַכְמֵיכֶם	זִקְנֵיכֶם	חַצְרֵיכֶם
Dual absol.	דְּבָרַיִם	חֲכָמַיִם	זִקְנַיִם	חֲצֵרַיִם

	IV.			V.
	Segolates with guttural			*Segolates of verb* ל"ה.
Sing. absol	נַעַר	נֶצַח	פֹּעַל	פְּרִי
— constr.	נַעַר	נֶצַח	פֹּעַל	פְּרִי
— with light suff.	נַעֲרִי	נצחי	פָּעֳלִי	פִּרְיִי
— with grave suff.	נַעַרְכֶם	נצחֲכֶם	פָּעָלְכֶם	פֶּרְיְכֶם
Plur. absol.	נְעָרִים	נְצָחִים	פְּעָלִים	פְּרָיִים
— (and dual) constr	נַעֲרֵי	נִצְחֵי	פָּעֳלֵי	etc.
— with light suff.	נְעָרַי	נִצְחַי	פָּעֳלַי	
— with grave suff	נַעֲרֵיכֶם	נצחיכֶם	פָּעֳלֵיכֶם	
Dual absol.	נַעֲרַיִם			

Declensions

II *Feminines with Kamets and Zerê.*			III. *Segolate forms.*		
שָׁנָה	צדקה	שׁנָה	מלֶךְ	ספֶר	קֹדֶשׁ
שׁנַת *	צדקת	שׁנַת	מלֶךְ	ספֶר	קֹדֶשׁ
שׁנָתִי	צדקתי	שׁנָתִי	מַלְכִּי	סִפְרִי	קָדְשִׁי
שׁנַתְכֶם	צדקתכם	שׁנַתְכֶם	מַלְכְּכֶם	סִפְרְכֶם	קָדְשְׁכֶם
שָׁנוֹת	צדקות	שׁנוֹת	מְלָכִים	סְפָרִים	קָדָשִׁים
שׁנוֹת	צדקות	שׁנוֹת	מַלְכִּי	סִפְרֵי	קָדְשֵׁי
שׁנוֹתַי	etc	etc	מַלְכַּי	סִפְרַי	קָדְשֵׁי
שׁנוֹתֵיכֶם			מַלְכֵיכֶם	סִפְרֵיכֶם	קָדְשֵׁיכֶם
שׁנָתַים			מַלְכַּים	סְפָרִים	קָדְשַׁים

	VI *Segolates of verb עו"*	VII *Participles*	VIII *Partic of verb ל"ה*	IX *Feminine segolates*		
	מָוֶת	מֹשֵׁל	חֹזֶה	מַלְכָּה	יוֹנֶקֶת	מַשְׂכֹּרֶת
	מוֹת	מֹשֵׁל	חֹזֶה	מַלְכַּת	יוֹנֶקֶת	מַשְׂכֹּרֶת
	מוֹתִי	מֹשְׁלִי	חֹזִי	מַלְכָּתִי	יוֹנַקְתִּי	מַשְׂכָּרְתִּי
	etc	מֹשֶׁלְכֶם	חֹזְכֶם	מַלְכַּתְכֶם	יוֹנַקְתְּכֶם	מַשְׂכָּרְתְּכֶם
of verb עו"		מֹשְׁלִים	חֹזִים	מַלְכוֹת	יוֹנְקוֹת	מַשְׂכְּרוֹת
absolut.	זַיִת	מֹשְׁלֵי	חֹזֵי	מַלְכוֹת	יוֹנְקוֹת	מַשְׂכְּרוֹת
constr.	זַיִת	מֹשְׁלֵי	חֹזֵי	מַלְכוֹתַי	יוֹנְקוֹתַי	מַשְׂכְּרוֹתַי
with suff	זַיְתִי	מֹשְׁלֵיכֶם	חֹזֵיכֶם	etc.	etc.	etc.
	etc					

---

*) In poetry sometimes with affix ־ִי, or ו v. g עָם רַבָּתִי instead of רַבַּת עָם *full of people,* חַיְתוֹ־אָרֶץ *the animals of the earth*

man), אֲנָשִׁים, constr. st. אַנְשֵׁי, which receives the suffixes of the plural

5. אָמָה *handmaid*, retains ה in the plural: אֲמָהוֹת, constr st אמהות

6 אִשָּׁה *woman;* constr st אֵשֶׁת, with suffixes as a se-golate אשת or אֶשְׁת, plur נָשִׁים (abbreviated form of אֲנָשִׁים).

7 בַּיִת *house;* constr st בית, plur. בָּתִּים (*bottîm*).

8 בֵּן *son;* constr. st בֶּן־ or בן־, joined by a Makkeph; plur בָּנִים, constr. st בְּנֵי; *my son* בני, *thy son* בנה, etc. plur with light suff. בַּי, with grave בניכם

9. בַּת *daughter;* plur בְּנוֹת, with suff. בתי, suff. of plur בנותיכם, בְּנוֹתַי

10 חָם *father in law*, and חֲמוֹת *mother in law* as אח and אָחוֹת.

11. יום *day*, plur יָמִים, constr st ימי

12 כְּלִי *a vase;* plur כלים

13. מַיִם *water;* constr st מֵי and מֵימֵי.

14. עִיר *city;* plur. עָרִים, constr. st. עָרֵי

15. פֶּה *mouth;* constr st פי, with suff פִּי *my mouth,* פיך *thy mouth.*

16 רֹאשׁ *head;* plur רָאשִׁים (*rashîm*).

§ 70. Participial forms.

For reference see paradigm, p 71, N VII and VIII

1 Participles are also true nouns and often in speech appear in the nature of substantives

2. The participles Kal, Piël, Hithpaël, by exception remain unchanged in the construct state of the singular, but when additions are made to the word, the Tserê of the last syllable undergoes various changes, v. g. שמר *watchman,* שמרי *my watchman,* שָׁמְרָךְ *thy watchman,* איבכם *your enemy.*

3. The participles of the verbs לה are apocopated (that is ה ָ is thrown out) before additions, v. g ראה *a prophet,* plur רֹאִים; מַרְאֶה *aspect,* with suff מַרְאֵהוּ. In the con-

struct state the Seghôl is lengthened into a Tserê רֹאֵה מִרְמָה
a prophet of fraud, that is, *a deceiving prophet*.

4 The participles of the verbs עֵ״ and עֵ״ו retain Kamets
or Tserê in the construct state, v g קָם, מֵת. Their femi-
nines do the same, v. g. קָמָה, constr. st קָמַת

Note - After the model of the participles which end in Tserê,
the Hebrew declines also the monosyllabic nouns that have Tserê for
vowel, as שֵם *name*, שְמִי *my name*, שִמְכֶם; עֵץ *wood*, עֵצִים, but cf § 68.

§ 71. Numerals.

1 The cardinal numbers are substantives, except אֶחָד
one, which has the nature of an adjective, and they are
irregular in their construction

No reason is known why the numerals from 3 to 10 have the
feminine form for the masculine gender and vice-versa

		Masculine		Feminine	
		Absol stat	Constr stat	Absol stat	Constr stat.
1	א	אֶחָד	אַחַד	אַחַת	אַחַת
2.	ב	שְׁנַיִם	שְׁנֵי	שְׁתַּיִם	שְׁתֵּי
3	ג	שְׁלֹשָׁה	שְׁלֹשֶׁת	שָׁלֹשׁ	שְׁלֹשׁ
4	ד	אַרְבָּעָה	אַרְבַּעַת	אַרְבַּע	אַרְבַּע
5.	ה	חֲמִשָּׁה	חֲמֵשֶׁת	חָמֵשׁ	חֲמֵשׁ
6	ו	שִׁשָּׁה	שֵׁשֶׁת	שֵׁשׁ	שֵׁשׁ
7.	ז	שִׁבְעָה	שִׁבְעַת	שֶׁבַע	שֶׁבַע
8.	ח	שְׁמֹנָה	שְׁמֹנַת	שְׁמֹנֶה	שְׁמֹנֶה
9	ט	תִּשְׁעָה	תִּשְׁעַת	תֵּשַׁע	תְּשַׁע
10.	י	עֲשָׂרָה	עֲשֶׂרֶת	עֶשֶׂר	עֶשֶׂר

		Masculine.		Feminine.	
11.	עָשָׂר יא	{	אַחַד / עַשְׁתֵּי	עֶשְׂרה {	אַחַת / עַשְׁתֵּי
12.	עָשָׂר יב	{	שְׁנֵי / שְׁנַיִם	עֶשְׂרה {	שְׁתֵּי / שְׁתֵּים

The manner of expressing the numbers from 13 to 19 is
to place the monads as separate words before עָשָׂר (fem.

עֲשָׂרֵה)), and to have the monads in the absolute state for the masculine gender and in the construct state for the feminine, v. g

13 יג שְׁלֹשָׁה עָשָׂר   שְׁלֹשׁ עֶשְׂרֵה
14 יד אַרְבָּעָה עָשָׂר   אַרְבַּע עֶשְׂרֵה etc to 19.

Twenty is signified by the plur. עֶשְׂרִים or by the letter כ The numerals from 30 to 90 are the plurals of the monads:

תשעים צ 90. שבעים ע 70. חֲמִשִׁים נ 50. שְׁלֹשִׁים ל 30.
אַרְבָּעִים מ 40. שִׁשִּׁים ס 60 שְׁמֹנִים פ 80 שִׁשִּׁים ס

All these decads have only one form, and have neither femin. nor constr. state. The monads are joined with them as separate words, either before them or, especially in latter books, after them. The monads and the decads are thus united by means of the conjunctive Vav which signifies *and:* עה, חֲמִשָּׁה ושבעים, *seventy-five*

A hundred: ק, מֵאָה, constr מֵאַת (subst. femin) *Two hundred:* ר, מָאתַיִם (dual). The following hundreds מֵאוֹת are joined to the monads which are in the constr. state of the femin, v. g. ש, שְׁלֹשׁ מֵאוֹת *three hundred*

A thousand: א, אֶלֶף (subst masc) *Two thousand,* ב, אַלְפַּיִם (dual). The other thousands are joined to the monads which are in the constr st of the masc., v g ד, אַרְבַּעַת אֲלָפִים *four thousand.* *Ten thousand* is expressed sometimes by רְבּוֹת (רִבּוֹ, רְבָבָה) that is, *multitudes.* *Twenty thousand* כ, רִבּוֹתַיִם (dual)

2. The ordinal numerals from *second* to *tenth* are formed from the cardinals, by adding ‏־ִי‎, and, besides, by placing another ‏־ִי‎ in the last syllable, except in שֵׁנִי and where there is already an *i* in the cardinal number Hence the forms:

שֵׁנִי *second*   חֲמִשִׁי *fifth* (also הַמִישִׁי)   שְׁמִינִי *eighth*
שְׁלִישִׁי *third*   שִׁשִּׁי *sixth*   תְּשִׁיעִי *ninth*
רְבִיעִי *fourth*   שְׁבִיעִי *seventh*   עֲשִׂירִי *tenth.*

First is רִאשׁוֹן (from ראש *beginning*), fem רִאשׁוֹנָה To form the femin of ordinals ת is added, v g שְׁמִינִית *eighth.*

The numbers above ten have no peculiar form of ordinals and for these the cardinals are used.

Note   The date of the months and the number of the years, even from one to ten, are expressed by the cardinal numbers, v g בִּשְׁנַת שָׁלוֹשׁ *in the third year*

3 Distributive numbers are expressed by means of repeated cardinals שְׁנַיִם שְׁנַיִם *two and two.*

4. Numeral adverbs are sometimes expressed by feminine cardinals: אַחַת *once*, שְׁתַּיִם *twice*, שָׁלוֹשׁ *three times*, but also by masculines, שִׁבְעִים וְשִׁבְעָה *seventy and sevenfold* More frequently, however, the substantive fem. פַּעַם *(step, stroke)* is added; *twice* is then expressed by the dual: פַּעֲמַיִם; *three times* שָׁלוֹשׁ פְּעָמִים, etc   The repetition of an action is rendered by the feminine forms of the cardinals: שֵׁנִית *a second time   Multiplicative adverbs* are expressed by the dual of the cardinals, v. g. אַרְבַּעְתַּיִם *fourfold*, שִׁבְעָתַיִם *sevenfold.*

5. Fractions are expressed by the feminine of ordinals, v g חֲמִישִׁית *the fifth part.*

6 Numerals also receive suffixes, v g שְׁנֵיהֶם *the two of them,* שְׁלָשְׁתְּכֶם *(sh⁼losht⁼chem) you three.*

D. The Particles.

§ 72. Adverbs.

1. Some adverbs take suffixes, and thus add to their meaning that of the substantive verb. Such suffixes are those of the verb, and include ordinarily the epenthetic Nûn, as the following:

אַיִן *not,* v. g. אֵינֶנִּי *I am not.*

יֵשׁ *present,* v g. יֶשְׁנוֹ *here he is*

עוֹד *still,* v. g. עוֹדֶנּוּ *he is still living.*

הִנֵּה *and* הֵן *behold,* v g. הִנְנִי *here I am, behold me, I am present,* הִנּוֹ *there he is.*

אֵי, *where,* v g. אַיּוֹ *where is he?* אַיֶּכָה *where art thou?*
אַיָּם *where are they?*

2. The interrogative particle is ordinarily הֲ, which
is joined as a prefix to the first word of a question, v. g
הֲשַׂמְתָּ לִבְּךָ לְעַבְדִּי אִיּוֹב *didst thou fix thy mind on my servant
Job?* Hence before consonants with a vocal Sh⁰vâ the
particle becomes הַ, v g. הַאֲנִי *do I?* הַשְׁמַעְתֶּם *have you
heard?* These consonants then often receive a Daghesh-forte
conjunctive, v g הַכְּתֹנֶת בִּנְךָ הִיא *is this the tunic of your
son?* Before gutturals it is either Pathach, v g. הַאִירָא *shall
I fear?* or Seghôl if they have Kamets, v g הֶחָכָם אַתָּה *art
thou wise?*

§ 73. Prepositions.

Some prepositions are no longer separate words, but
truncated forms which are attached as prefixes to the word
they govern   Among these are especially בְּ *in,* כְּ *like,*
לְ *to,* the use of which has been explained above (§ 53);
also מִן, which is generally joined to its word (§ 16; 11, 2
and also 53).

Note   The word יְהוָֹה is never pronounced by the Jews   In
its stead they read אֲדֹנָי   Hence these prepositions before יְהוָֹה are
marked with the vowel that would be required by the form אֲדֹנָי : לַיהוָֹה.

§ 74. Suffixes of prepositions (cases of personal
pronouns).

1. Since prepositions are true nouns, they can also be
augmented with suffixes, viz. of the noun, v. g. תַּחַת (*under*
or *in place of, for*) with a suffix תַּחְתִּי *in my place*   When
the preposition אֵת (*with, by*) has suffixes, it is distinguished
from אֵת, the sign of the accusative, by having the preposition changed into אִתּ (for אֵנְת), while the note of the
accusative passes into אֹת (אוֹת), v g אִתִּי *with me,* אֹתִי *me.*

2. Here we must principally note the prepositions,
enumerated in the preceding paragraph, because, when they

are joined to suffixed pronouns, they return to their primitive form, and also follow the rule given at § 18, 3
(in regard to taking a Kamets)

	לִי	to me	אֹתִי	me		בִּי	in me
m.	לְךָ‎} (in pause לָךְ)		אֹתְךָ‎} thee		m.	בְּךָ	etc.
f.	לָךְ‎} to thee		אֹתָךְ		f.	בָּךְ	
m.	לוֹ	to him	אֹתוֹ	him		בּוֹ	
f.	לָהּ	to her	אֹתָהּ	her		בָּהּ	
	לָנוּ	to us	אֹתָנוּ	us		בָּנוּ	
	לָכֶם‎-ן	to you	אֶתְכֶם‎-ן	you		בָּכֶם‎-ן	
	לָהֶם‎-ן	to them	אֹתָם‎-ן	them		בָּהֶם‎-ן (בָּם‎-ן)	

	מִמֶּנִּי	by me		כָּמוֹנִי	like me
	מִמְּךָ‎} by thee			כָּמוֹךָ	like thee
	מִמֶּךָ‎}		m.	כָּמוֹהוּ	etc.
	מִמֶּנּוּ	by him	f.	כָּמוֹהָ	
	מִמֶּנָּה	by her		כָּמוֹנוּ	
	מִמֶּנּוּ	by us		כְּמוֹכֶם‎-ן	
	מִכֶּם‎-ן‎} by you			כָּכֶם‎-ן	
	מִנְהֶם‎-ן‎}			כְּמוֹהֶם‎-ן	
	מֵהֶם‎-ן	by them		כָּהֶם‎-ן	

Besides these forms, the poets use also: לָמוֹ *to them,*
מֶּנִּי and מֶּנִּי *by me,* מִנְהוּ and מִפֵּהוּ *by him.*

Note   In poetry also appear the forms לָמוֹ, בְּמוֹ and כְּמוֹ for
לְ, בְּ, כְּ without suffixes as separate words

3. There are prepositions which have a plural form and
therefore receive the suffixes of the plural   Others appear
indifferently as singular and as plural nouns   Such are:

אַחַר *after,*   with suff. אַחֲרֶיךָ *after thee*
אֶל *to, in*   „   „   אֵלֶיךָ *to thee*
בֵּין *between*   „   „   בֵּינֶיךָ *between thee*

בֵּין appears also in the plural form בֵּינוֹת, v. g בֵּינוֹתָם
between them.

Sometimes, and chiefly in poetical books, the prepo-

sitions מִן *from, by,* עַד *until,* עַל *over,* and תַּחַת *under,*
are also used in the plural: מִנֵּי, עֲדֵי, עֲלֵי and תַּחְתֵּי, and
hence they likewise take the suffixes of the plural: מִנֶּיךָ
from thee, עָדַי *to me,* עֲלֵיהֶם *over them* (also עָלֵימוֹ), and
תַּחְתָּיו *under him* or *in his stead*

§ 75. Conjunctions.

1. The conjunction most frequently used is the so called
conjunctive Vav. It is in fact used to connect both words
and sentences, which are bound together in any manner, so
that it expresses various ideas of connection. As such it
has a vocal Sh⁰vâ, which however may be replaced by
various vowels according to the rules given above, especially in § 18. We note here, however, that the conjunctive
Vav is written with a Shûrek when a) it precedes a vocal
Sh⁰vâ; b) before any of the labial letters בומף. Thus arise
the forms וִיהִי for וְיִהְיֶה, וְהָיָה for וֶהֱיֶה, וַעֲמֹד, וּלֹה, וְגֹם,
טוֹב וָרַע, וּבְאָרֶץ.

The other conjunctions will be found in the lexicon.
We observe only that by the addition of the relative
particle אֲשֶׁר many prepositions become conjunctions, v. g.
כַּאֲשֶׁר *as (quemadmodum),* אַחַר אֲשֶׁר *after (postquam),* עַד
אֲשֶׁר *until* etc.

§ 76. Interjections.

Besides the properly called interjections הוֹי, אֲהָהּ, אָהּ,
many other parts of speech, when uttered with great viva-
city, become also interjections, v. g. הֵן and הִנֵּה *behold!*
הָבָה, plur. הָבוּ *do* (imper. of יָהַב), לְכָה and לְכוּ (also imper.
of יָלַךְ *to go*) *go away!* etc. Particles of obsecration are
בִּי and נָא (*I pray*).

Chapter Third.
Syntax.

A. Syntax of the nouns.

§ 77. The article.

1. The Hebrew often omits the article where our languages require it Thus the article is never joined to a word which has a suffix, or which is in the construct state, v. g. בְּנֵי הָאֶבְיוֹן *the children of the poor (man)*.

2. The article, placed before the genitive, belongs to the governing noun, or rather to the whole compound sentence, v. g. בֵּית הַמֶּלֶךְ *the house of the king*, whereas בֵּית מֶלֶךְ means *a kingly house*.

3. When the substantive takes the article, it is likewise taken by the adjective and the demonstrative pronoun, which qualify and determine the substantive, v. g. הָעֵצָה הָרָעָה *the bad advice*, הַגּוֹי הַגָּדוֹל הַזֶּה *this great people*.

4. All such epithets require the article, even when their substantive omits it, on account only of having a suffix or a genitive (cfr n. 1) בֵּית הַמֶּלֶךְ הַגָּדוֹל *the great house of the king*.

5. Proper nouns do not take the article, except such as are properly appellative or common, and in which the emphasis of the article must show that they are used as proper nouns, v g. הַלְּבָנוֹן *Mount Lebanon, the White (Mountain)*, הָרָמָה *the city of Rama (the high place)*.

6. The article sometimes has a demonstrative power, especially הַפַּעַם *this time*, הַיּוֹם *(this day), today*.

7. The vocative is ordinarily expressed by means of the article, v. g. הַמֶּלֶךְ *o king!* הַכֹּהֵן הַגָּדוֹל *o high priest!*

8. The Hebrew article is also written where it is not the individuality of a person or a thing, but the singular

number of the species which is to be designated, v g.
כַּשֶּׁלֶג יַלְבִּינוּ *they may become white as snow*, כָּבֵד בַּמִּקְנֶה
בַּכֶּסֶף וּבַזָּהָב *rich in flocks, in silver and in gold.*

9 The indefinite article of modern languages is either
not expressed at all, or its place is sometimes filled by the
numeral אֶחָד (one), v. g וְהִנֵּה נָבִיא אֶחָד נִגַּשׁ אֶל־אַחְאָב *and,
behold, a prophet approached Achab.*

§ 78. Genders.

The Hebrew having but two genders, the masculine
and the feminine, the latter is used in the sense of our
neuter to express abstract and general notions, v. g אֵין בּוֹ
נְכוֹחָה *there is in him nothing right* (fem of adj נָכוֹחַ),
Ps XXVI, 4. אַחַת שָׁאַלְתִּי *one thing I asked.* The Vulgate
retained the feminine: *unam petii, hanc requiram.*

§ 79. Numbers.

1. The singular is often used to express all, collectively
taken, as בָּקָר *the oxen* (drove of oxen), צֹאן *the flocks*, עֵץ
the timbers, the forest, כֶּסֶף *the silver, the money.* Should
these collectives occur in the plural, they then have a
different signification, v. g חִטִּים *grains of wheat,* כְּסָפִים
pieces of silver. The singular of names of nations with the
article has often the force of the plural, v. g. הַיְבוּסִי *the
Jebusites.*

2. Pluralis majestaticus   The plural is in some
cases used in Hebrew to indicate reverence, when there is
question of one person only. This peculiarity is called the
majestic plural, as is seen in the following words:

אֱלֹהִים *God*, plural of אֱלוֹהַּ. This name is generally
used for the true God, rarely for the gods of the gentiles.

אֲדֹנָי (an obsolete form of plural) and אֲדֹנִים *Lord*
(constr st. אֲדֹנֵי, singular אָדוֹן). God is always expressed

by the form אֲדֹנָי, whereas a powerful man is designated
by the form אֲדֹנָי *my lords* (for אֲדֹנִי *my lord*)

Note The Jews, out of reverence, did not pronounce the proper
name of God as it had been revealed to Moses, but read in its stead,
when meeting it in the Bible, אֲדֹנָי Hence the punctuators sub-
scribed also to the consonants יחוה the vowels of the word *'ᵃdhonay*,
אֲדֹנָי In Jehova, however, there is a simple Shᵉvâ, because Yôdh is
not a guttural like א Should it happen that אֲדֹנָי is already in
conjunction with יחוה, the Jews pronounce it *'ᵉlohîm*, and therefore
place the vowels of the word אלהים under יחוה, v g כֹּה אָמַר אֲדֹנָי
יחוה (read: *co 'amar 'ᵃdhonay 'ᵉlohîm*) The proper punctuation of the
name of God, which has been lost by disuse, seems to be יַהְוֶה *Jahve*
(Fut of הָוָה, which form, used in Aramaic, is rare in Hebrew for הָיָה
he was) and thus means *who will be* or *who is*, that is the Eternal

שַׁדַּי *the Almighty*, old plural form of שֵׁד.

קְדוֹשִׁים *the most Holy*, plural of קָדוֹשׁ

בַּעַל *lord, master*, if it has a suffix, is ordinarily placed
in the plural with the force of the singular, v g בְּעָלָיו
his master, בְּעָלֶיהָ *her master*. Yet the plural of this word
frequently still has its original power, v g בַּעֲלֵי גוים *the
lords of the nations*

3 The plural is used also to place greater stress on
the notion, v. g נְקָמוֹת (full) *vengeance*

4 There are, besides, many nouns that occur in the
plural only: some of them because abstract notions are
expressed in Hebrew by means of the plural, v g חַיִּים
life, זְקֻנִים *old age*, רַחֲמִים *mercy*, etc ; others for peculiar
reasons, v. g צַוָּארִים *neck* (because there are two bones),
פָּנִים *face*, plur of פָּנֶה *cheek*, אוֹדוֹת *moments*, לוּלִים *spoon*,
מְתִים *men, mortals*, כַּוָּנִים *cake*.

5 When a notion, composed of a substantive and a
genitive, is to be expressed in the plural, ordinarily the
construct state alone becomes plural, v g גִּבּוֹרֵי חַיִל *heroes
of strength, strong heroes;* sometimes the two words are placed
in the plural, v g גִּבּוֹרֵי חֲיָלִים; rarely the genitive alone,
v. g בֵּית אָבוֹת *families*

§ 80. The cases.

a) Nominative

Nominative absolute. In Hebrew a word is placed
sometimes at the beginning of a sentence, and is even joined
with the following words by a conjunctive Vav, without
governing any verb in the sentence, and this is done in
order to attract the attention and to enliven the speech.
Such a noun is said to be in the nominative absolute.
Its relation with the sentence is indicated by pronouns,
v g לַיִשׁ גִּבּוֹר הוּא בַּבְּהֵמָה *the lion, he is strong among the
animals,* יהוה בַּשָּׁמַיִם כִּסְאוֹ *the Lord, his throne is in heaven;*
occasionally ו joins the nominative absolute with the rest,
v g שָׁנָיו וְלֹא חֵקֶר לָהֶם *his years, and there is no number
to them.*

b) Genitive

The use of the construct state is much more extensive
than that of the genitive proper It is used:

1 Where we have apposition, v. g. נְהַר פְּרָת *the river
Euphrates,* בְּתוּלַת בַּת־יְהוּדָה *virgin, daughter of Juda.*

2. Where the foundation of the dependence is either
in the object (objective genitive) as יִרְאַת יהוה *the fear of
the Lord*, or in the subject (subjective genitive), אַף יְהוָה
the anger of the Lord.

3. Where the notion of the adjective is determined
by the addition of a noun, v. g נְקִי כַפַּיִם *pure of hands,*
יְפֵה מַרְאֶה *beautiful of aspect.*

4 Where, instead of an adjective, a noun expressing
the quality is added, v g שֵׁבֶט מִישׁוֹר *a sceptre of justice =
a just sceptre,* כְּלֵי כֶסֶף וּכְלֵי זָהָב *vases of silver and vases
of gold = silver and gold vases,* סֵפֶל אַדִּירִים *vial of magni-
ficences = a magnificent vial,* כְּלִי נחֹשֶׁת *vases of brass,* תֵּבַת
עֵצִים *an ark of wood.*

5 The construct state, moreover, is used before prepositions, principally בְּ, because they were originally

nouns, v. g. יֹשְׁבֵי בְאֶרֶץ צַלְמָוֶת *dwelling (dwellers) in the land of the shadow of death*, שִׂמְחַת בַּקָּצִיר *joy in the harvest..*

6. Sometimes before אֲשֶׁר, v g מְקוֹם אֲשֶׁר יִשְׁחַט *the place where they immolate.*

7. Seldom before the conjunctive Vav, v g חָכְמַת וָדָעַת *wisdom and knowledge*

8. In the composition of numerals, concerning which see § 71

c) Other forms with the power of the genitive.

Besides the construct state, there are two other ways in Hebrew of expressing the genitive:

1 אֲשֶׁר לְ (relative with dative), v. g הָרֹעִים אֲשֶׁר לְשָׁאוּל *the shepherds of Saul (who are to Saul);* this is the ordinary way of expressing the possessive genitive

2. לְ alone, with אֲשֶׁר understood, v g. בֶּן לִישָׁי *the son of Isai* This form is principally used when one genitive depends on another, v g. דִּבְרֵי יָמִים לְמַלְכֵי יִשְׂרָאֵל *the words of the days (the history) of the kings of Israel* Also where the time is indicated by numbers, this form of the genitive is ordinarily used, v. g בְּשִׁבְעָה וְעֶשְׂרִים יוֹם לַחֹדֶשׁ, *on the 27th day of the month* Frequently in the same manner is the Lamedh in use which is called the Lamedh of the author, v g מִזְמוֹר לְדָוִיד *a psalm of David,* a passive construction where לְ has the power of the English preposition *by* with כָּתוּב understood: *a psalm written by David.*

d) Dative

1 The dative is used in Hebrew with the passive verb to signify the subject of the active, v g. בָּרוּךְ לַיהוָֹה *blessed by the Lord,* Par. Sal. XIV, 20, נֵם לְרֵעֵהוּ יִשָּׂנֵא רָשׁ *the poor man is odious to (hated by) even his companion*

2 Verbs, which in Latin take a double accusative or nominative, have the one, expressing the notion of the pre-

dicate, in the dative without the article, v g. Job XVII, 12,
לַיְלָה לְיוֹם יָשִׂימוּ *they turned the night into day*, 2. Kings V, 3,
וַיִּמְשְׁחוּ אֶת־דָּוִד לְמֶלֶךְ *they anointed David king*, 1. Kings IV, 9,
הֱיוּ לַאֲנָשִׁים *be ye men*.

e) Accusative

1. **Adverbial accusative** The accusative, besides
expressing the object, is often used adverbially to indicate
the time, measure, place, manner, etc, v g נֵצֵא הַשָּׂדֶה *let
us go out into the fields*, הַיּוֹם *to day*, פֶּה אֶחָד *with one
voice (mouth), one accord*

2. Nouns, derived from transitive verbs, prefer the
accusative to the genitive, as if they were still participles
or infinitives, v g יְרֵא אֶת יהוה *fearing the Lord* (the fearer
of), דֵּעָה אֶת יהוה *the knowledge of the Lord*

3 The accusative with אֵת is sometimes the subject
of a passive verb, v g וְלֹא יִקָּרֵא עוֹד אֶת־שְׁמֵךְ *and your
name shall no more be pronounced*

§ 81. Apposition.

Appositions, that is, the connection of two nouns
in the absolute state, are found in Hebrew not only where
other languages use them, but sometimes also where the
genitive is expected, v. g כִּכָּרַיִם כָּסֶף *two talents of silver,*
הַמַּבּוּל מַיִם *the deluge of water*

§ 82. Repetition of nouns.

A noun, repeated twice or three times without any
intervening word, signifies:

1. a **multitude**, v. g בְּאֵרוֹת בְּאֵרוֹת *wells next to wells;*
2 **universality**, v g יוֹם יוֹם *every day*, אִישׁ אִישׁ
to a man (every one), דּוֹר וָדוֹר *all generations;*
3 **distribution**, v g בַּבֹּקֶר בַּבֹּקֶר *one morning after
another;*

4 variety, v. g. וָאֶבֶן לֹה אֶבֶן יִהְיֶה לֹא *you shall not have double (different) weights;* לֵב וָלֵב *heart and heart,* that is, *double-hearted.*

§ 83. Syntax of the adjectives.

A Comparative

The comparative degree in Hebrew has no peculiar form of its own, but is expressed by placing the particle מִן (as a prefix מ·) after the adjective in the positive form and before the noun with which the comparison is instituted. Thus v. g חָכָם מִמֶּלֶךְ *wiser than the king (wise before the king),* מָתוֹק מִדְּבַשׁ *sweeter than honey.* This construction, moreover, denotes also superabundance and excess, and is therefore used likewise after verbs which indicate a quality, v g הַדָּבָר אֲשֶׁר יִקְשֶׁה מִכֶּם *the affair which will be too difficult for you;* this comparative מִן is especially used before infinitives, v g גָּדוֹל עֲוֹנִי מִנְּשׂוֹא *my crime is too great to be taken away.*

B Superlative

The superlative also has no proper form, and is expressed by some circumlocution. Its function is filled either by the article placed before the adjective, v g. דָּוִד הוּא הַקָּטָן *David was the smallest* (youngest), or by adding the particle מְאֹד, even repeated, v g Num XIV, 7, טוֹבָה הָאָרֶץ מְאֹד מְאֹד *the land is very good,* or also by repetition of the adjective, v. g. קָדוֹשׁ קָדוֹשׁ קָדוֹשׁ *holy, holy, holy — most holy.*

C Connection of adjectives with their substantives

1 An adjective, which is an epithet or qualificative, is placed after the substantive which it qualifies, and it agrees with this substantive in gender, number and article; v g. הַגּוֹי הַגָּדוֹל *the great nation.*

2. The majestic plural ordinarily takes adjectives in the singular, v g אֲדֹנִים קָשֶׁה *a cruel master*

3 Collective nouns have their adjectives and participles in the plural, v g הָעָם הַהֹלְכִים בַּחֹשֶׁךְ *the people walking in darkness.*

4 The dual has plural adjectives and participles, v. g. יָדַיִם רָפוֹת *weary hands.*

5 Adjectives, when predicates, are placed before the substantive without the article, and the "copula" is generally omitted, v g גָּדוֹל הָאֱלֹהִים *God is great,* זֶה אֱלֹהֶיךָ *this is your God;* but we find also גְדוֹלָה הָיְתָה נִינְוֵה *Ninive was large*

§ 84. Syntax of the numerals.

The cardinal numerals from two to ten are sometimes used as substantives and sometimes as adverbs   Hence they are joined with the object, which is qualified by the number, in a threefold manner: 1. in the construct state before the substantive; 2 also before, in the absolute state; 3 after the substantive, in the absolute state, this principally in the latter books written in Hebrew, v g שְׁלֹשָׁה יָמִים or שְׁלֹשֶׁת יָמִים or יָמִים שְׁלֹשָׁה *three days*

2 The monads ordinarily take their substantive in the plural, v. g שֶׁבַע פָּרוֹת *seven cous,* בָּנוֹת שָׁלוֹשׁ *three daughters;* the decads generally in the singular, if they precede, but in the plural, if they follow, v g תִּשְׁעִים אַמָּה *ninety cubits,* אֵילִים עֶשְׂרִים *twenty rams*   The same construction is used for numbers composed of monads and decads, v. g חֲמֵשׁ עֶשְׂרֵה אַמּוֹת *fifteen cubits,* אַחַת וְשֵׁשׁ מֵאוֹת שָׁנָה *six hundred and one years*   Sometimes the object itself is added twice to these compound numerals, and this in the plural to the monad and in the singular to the decad, v g חָמֵשׁ שָׁנִים וְשִׁשִּׁים שָׁנָה *sixty-five years*

3 The ordinals follow entirely the syntax of adjectives (§ 83), v. g. הַיּוֹם הַשֵּׁנִי *the second day,* שֵׁנִי דָנִיֵּאל *Daniel was the second.*

§ 85. Syntax of the pronouns.

A The personal pronoun

1 The separate pronoun often includes the verb sub-stantive or simply expresses the same, v. g חָכָם גַּם הוּא *he too is wise,* מְרַגְּלִים אַתֶּם *you are spies* The separate pronoun of the third person serves also as *copula* between the subject and the predicate, v. g זֶה מַתַּת אֱלֹהִים הִיא *this is a gift of God,* מָה הֵמָּה אֵלֶּה *what are those?* גַּם־זֶה הוּא רַעְיוֹן רוּחַ *this is also an affliction of the spirit* This is the case even where the subject is in the first or second person, v g אַתָּה־הוּא יְהוָה *thou art the Lord,* רְאוּ עַתָּה כִּי אֲנִי אֲנִי הוּא *see now that it is I, I myself.*

2 The separate pronoun is sometimes found after a suffix of the same person, with or without גַּם, v g אַתָּה הוֹדַעְתִּיךְ *I have made thee known,* בָּרְכֵנִי גַם אָנִי *bless me also,* לִבִּי גַם אָנִי *my heart also,* נַפְשׁוֹ הוּא *his soul,* לָכֶם אַתֶּם *to you,* וַתְּהִי עָלָיו גַם־הוּא רוּחַ אֱלֹהִים *and the Spirit of God came into him also*

3. The suffix of the verb ordinarily denotes the accu-sative, yet with intransitive verbs it has also the power of the dative, v g גְּדֵלַנִי כְאָב *he grew to me as to a father,* אֶרֶץ הַנֶּגֶב נְתַתָּנִי *thou hast given me the southern land*

4 When the verb receives two accusatives of a pro-noun, the one is attached as a suffix, the other follows as a separate pronoun, connected by אֵת, v g. הִרְאַנִי אֹתוֹ *he made me see him, he showed him to me.*

5. The suffix of the noun may be either the objective or the subjective genitive Thus יִרְאָתוֹ is either *his fear* or *the fear of him,* חֲמָסִי *my injury (to somebody or from somebody).*

6 When a notion, compounded of a noun and a genitive, demands a suffix, it is the genitive that receives it, v g. כְּלֵי מִלְחַמְתּוֹ *his instruments of war, his arms,* הַר קָדְשִׁי *my holy mountain.*

B The demonstrative pronoun

1 The pronoun זֶה has sometimes the power of the
relative (chiefly in poetical books), v g הַר צִיּוֹן זֶה שָׁכַנְתָּ בּוֹ
the mount of Sion on which thou dwellest, שְׁמַע לְאִמְּךָ זֶה יְלָדַתְךָ
obey thy mother who bore thee

2. The demonstrative of a substantive, which has an
adjective, follows the latter, v g. הָהָר הַגָּדוֹל הַזֶּה this great
mountain.

3 הוּא, when used as a demonstrative, means himself,
v. g. אֲדֹנָי הוּא the Lord himself Joined with the article,
the pronouns הוּא and הִיא are used to express the same,
this and that, v. g בָּעֵת הַהִיא at this same time, הַיּוֹם הַזֶּה
this day, הַיּוֹם הַהוּא on that day, at the same time, הַגּוֹיִם
הַגְּדֹלִים הָאֵלֶּה those great nations

C The interrogative pronoun

1. The interrogative pronoun מָה sometimes expresses
no interrogation and signifies something, v. g Prov IX, 13
בַּל־יָדְעָה־מָּה she cares nothing; or also whatever, II Kings
XVIII, 22, וִיהִי מָה אָרוּצָה howsoever, I shall run; more
frequently, however, מְאוּמָה is used in these senses.

2. Moreover מָה is joined to prepositions in various
ways: לָמָּה or לָמָה, amplified לָמָה־זֶּה why? כַּמָּה how many,
how often? בַּמָּה in what, for what? עַד־מָה to where, how
far? עַל־מָה what for? why?

3. מָה is also used adverbially, v g Ps VIII, 2 מָה־אַדִּיר
שִׁמְךָ how admirable is thy name; Num XXIV, 5 מַה־טֹּבוּ
אֹהָלֶיךָ how beautiful are thy tabernacles.

4 The particle אֵי placed before the demonstrative pronoun makes the interrogative adjective (what? qualis?),
v g. Esth. VII, 5 מִי הוּא זֶה וְאֵי־זֶה הוּא who is this, and
what is he? אֵי־זֶה הַדֶּרֶךְ הָלָךְ what way did he go? אֵי מִזֶּה
עִיר אַתָּה from what city art thou?

D The relative pronoun

1. As אֲשֶׁר is now a pronoun, then a simple note of relation, and then again a conjunction, the following observations will help to show its meaning.

2 The nominative and the accusative of the relative pronoun are expressed by the simple term אֲשֶׁר, v. g. כָּל־אֲשֶׁר־לוֹ *all he had,* מְלַאכְתּוֹ אֲשֶׁר עָשָׂה *his work which he had done.*

Note Here is to be noted the passage of Gen XLV, 4, אֲנִי יוֹסֵף אֲחִיכֶם אֲשֶׁר מְכַרְתֶּם אֹתִי, where the accusative אֲשֶׁר receives, in addition, the separate pronoun of the first person: *I am Joseph, your brother, whom you sold (me)*

3 Most frequently אֲשֶׁר includes also the antecedent pronoun (like the English *what* for *that which*), v g אֲשֶׁר לֹא שָׁמְעוּ הִתְבּוֹנָנוּ *those, who heard not, understood* This occurs always when אֲשֶׁר is coupled with a preposition, v g לַאֲשֶׁר *to him, who* or *to her, who* etc , מֵאֲשֶׁר *from him, who,* אֶת־אֲשֶׁר *him, who;* Gen. XLIII, 16 וַיֹּאמֶר לַאֲשֶׁר עַל בֵּיתוֹ *he said to the one who (was) over his household;* III Kings X, 13 מִלְּבַד אֲשֶׁר נָתַן לָה, *besides what he had given her.* Thus also Ruth I, 16, אֶל־אֲשֶׁר תֵּלְכִי אֵלֵךְ, *wherever thou goest, I will go*

4 Commonly אֲשֶׁר is only a mark of relation which connects the secondary with the principal proposition. Hence adverbs and pronouns, whenever joined with אֲשֶׁר, become relatives; v g שָׁם *there,* אֲשֶׁר .. שָׁם *where,* שָׁמָּה *thither,* אֲשֶׁר .. שָׁמָּה *whither,* מִשָּׁם *thence,* אֲשֶׁר ... מִשָּׁם *whence,* אֲשֶׁר .. אוֹתוֹ *whom.* The indirect cases, therefore, of the relative pronoun are expressed in Hebrew by joining אֲשֶׁר with the suffixes of the pronouns and the signs of the cases, yet not in such a way as to change the order of the words, viz

Gen. אֲשֶׁר אָזְנוֹ *whose ear,* אֲשֶׁר־תַּחַת־כְּנָפָיו *under whose wings.*

Dat. כֹּל אֲשֶׁר־לוֹ סְנַפִּיר *all to which there are scales,* הָאֲנָשִׁים אֲשֶׁר לָהֶם הָרִיב *men, who have a quarrel.*

Acc. הַפֹּץ אֲשֶׁר תִּדְּפֶנּוּ רוּחַ *the dust, which the wind scatters.*

Abl הָאָרֶץ אֲשֶׁר נָרוּ בָהּ *the land in which they dwelt,* רָעָה אֲשֶׁר לֹא יוּכְלוּ לָצֵאת מִמֶּנָּה *the evil from which they could not rid themselves*

Note   An ancient and poetical construction uses זֶה in a like and indeclinable manner, v g הַר־זֶה קָנְתָה יְמִינוּ *the mountain which his right hand acquired,* הַר צִיּוֹן זֶה שָׁכַנְתָּ בּוֹ *Mount Sion, on which thou dwellest*   (Vulg · *Mons Sion in quo habitasti in eo*)

5. In whichever of the described ways אֲשֶׁר could be used, it may be omitted and understood as in English, v g. אֱלֹ־יִדְרֹךְ יִדְרֹךְ הַדּרֵךְ לֹא יָדְעוּ *on a way they knew not,* קַשְׁתּוֹ *against (him who) bends, let him who bends, bend his bow,* גְּזַל שְׁאוֹל חָטָאוּ *hell devoured (those who) sinned,* אָדָם לֹא יַחְשֹׁב יְהוָה לוֹ עָוֹן *the man God did not impute sin to.* Whence also שָׂפַת לֹא יָדַעְתִּי *the tongue (of him) I knew not,* שְׁלַח־נָא בְּיַד תִּשְׁלָח *send I pray by means (of him) thou art to send.*

6. When אֲשֶׁר is used as a conjunction, it has many meanings, concerning which the dictionary should be consulted   Hence, we should only observe here that when אשר begins an objective proposition, it is sometimes preceded by the sign of the accusative, v g זְכָר־נָא אֵת אֲשֶׁר הִתְהַלַּכְתִּי לְפָנֶיךָ בֶּאֱמֶת *remember, I pray, that I walked before thee in truth.*

7 The indefinite relative pronoun is מִי אֲשֶׁר *whoever,* v. g. מִי אֲשֶׁר חָטָא לִי אֶמְחֶנּוּ מִסִּפְרִי *whoever sins against me, I will wipe him out of my book.*

E The reflexive, numeral and reciprocal pronouns

1. The reflexive pronoun is rendered in Hebrew by means of the conjugations Niphal and Hithpaël, or by the suffix of the third person, or by some circumlocution expressing the soul, the heart, the flesh, etc. of the agent, v g הָיוּ רֹעִים אוֹתָם *they were feeding themselves,* לֹא אֵדַע נַפְשִׁי

I do not know myself, אַל תַּשְׁאוּ נַפְשֹׁתֵיכֶם *do not defraud yourselves.*

2. The reciprocal pronoun is signified by the circumlocution of *brother* or *neighbor*, even when there is question of inanimate objects, v. g. לֹא רָאוּ אִישׁ אֶת־אָחִיו *they did not see one another,* וַיֹּאמְרוּ אִישׁ אֶל־רֵעֵהוּ *and they said to each other,* כַּנְפֵי הַחַיּוֹת מַשִּׁיקוֹת אִשָּׁה אֶל־אֲחוֹתָהּ *the wings of the animals struck one against the other.* The disjunctive is זֶה—זֶה *the one ... the other,* v. g. וְקָרָא זֶה אֶל־זֶה *and the one cried to the other.*

3 *Each, every one* is expressed by אִישׁ and אִשָּׁה or אִישׁ אִישׁ, or אִישׁ וָאִישׁ, v. g אִישׁ מִמֶּנּוּ *every one of us,* כִּרְצוֹן אִישׁ וָאִישׁ *according to everybody's wish.*

4 *Somebody, some one* is likewise אִישׁ or אָדָם or כֹּל; *something, anything* is מְאוּמָה, כָּל־דָּבָר, כֹּל, דָּבָר, v. g. כִּי יִהְיֶה בָּאָרֶץ כָּל־נֶגַע וְכָל־מַחֲלָה *shall there be any trouble or any disease on earth,* הֲיִפָּלֵא מֵיהוָה דָּבָר *shall any thing be difficult for the Lord?* By adding to these words a form of negation, they express *no one* and *nothing,* v g לֹא אוּכַל לַעֲשׂוֹת דָּבָר *I can do nothing,* אֵין כָּל־חָדָשׁ תַּחַת הַשָּׁמֶשׁ *there is nothing new under the sun,* אֵין אִישׁ עִמָּנוּ *there is nobody with us,* לֹא נִמְלַט מֵהֶם אִישׁ *not one of them escaped,* לֹא יָשׁוּב לֹא־נוֹתַר כֹּל יָרָק *he does not recede from anybody,* מִפְּנֵי־כֹל *nothing green remained* *Some* are called אֲחָדִים or יֵשׁ אֲשֶׁר, v g. יָשַׁבְתָּ עִמּוֹ יָמִים אֲחָדִים, *you remained with him some days,* יֵשׁ אֲשֶׁר אֹמְרִים *some were saying.*

B Syntax of the verbs

§ 86. Use of the tenses.

1. The perfect has generally the same power as the historical perfect of the Latin, *amavit,* including both the imperfect and perfect of the English, for it is a narrative tense It is less frequently used in the sense of the Latin imperfect, *amabat* (he was loving) and pluperfect,

v. g. Job I, 1 אִישׁ הָיָה בְאֶרֶץ עִיץ *there was a man in the land of Hus*, Gen. II, 5 לֹא הִמְטִיר יְהֹוָה *the Lord had not yet made it rain*

2 The perfect has furthermore the power of the conditional mode and of the imperfect and pluperfect of the subjunctive, v. g לוּלֵא יְהֹוָה הוֹתִיר לוּ מַתְנוּ *if we had died*, לָנוּ שָׂרִיד כִּסְדֹם הָיִינוּ *had the Lord not left us a remnant, we should have been like Sodom* (Is I, 9)

3. The perfect is used even for the present, where it indicates a steady habit, principally in common and universal declarations as are found in moral books, in proverbs and in psalms, v g. אָמַר עָצֵל גּוּר בַחוּץ *the lazy man says: there is a lion on the road*, גָדַלְתָּ יְהֹוָה *thou art great, o Lord.*

4 The future or imperfect usually indicates whatever action or state is unfinished First, therefore, it signifies the future time; then it is also put for the present, mostly when something is declared that is perpetual, general, moral, v g. לֹא יִהְיֶה עוֹד מַבּוּל *no more will there be a deluge*, לֹא יוּכְלוּן הַמִּצְרִים לָאֱכֹל אֶת־הָעִבְרִים לָחֶם *the Egyptians are not allowed to eat bread with the Hebrews*, יִרְאַת יְהֹוָה תּוֹסִיף יָמִים *the fear of God adds days (to life)*

5. In a spirited discourse the future is even used for the perfect, especially where an action or a custom is spoken of, that is continued afterwards: כָּכָה יַעֲשֶׂה אִיּוֹב כָּל־הַיָּמִים *Job would do so all the time* Sometimes it is seen from the addition of the particles אָז *then*, and בְּטֶרֶם *before (that)* that the future is to be understood as a perfect, v g אָז אָז יְדַבֵּר יְהוֹשֻׁעַ לַיהֹוָה *then said Josue to the Lord*, אָז יַעֲלֶה חֲזָאֵל *then did Hazael go up*, מֵשִׁיב דָּבָר בְּטֶרֶם יִשְׁמָע אִוֶּלֶת הִיא לוֹ *he who answers before he heard, this is a folly to him (is foolish).*

§ 87. The subjunctive.

The future is used in Hebrew for the subjunctive, and the same has often the power of the imperative; it is even

more frequently used to signify the subjunctive than the
future. Thus the future has the power of the subjunctive
after final conjunctions, v g לְמַעַן תְּבָרֶכְךָ נַפְשִׁי *that I may
bless thee,* פֶּן־תִּכְרֹת בְּרִית *do not make a covenant;* also in
expressing wishes, precepts, prayers, exhortations and in
declaring power, permission, will, v. g יֹאבַד יוֹם אִוָּלֶד בּוֹ
let the day perish wherein I was born, יְדַבֶּר־נָא עַבְדְּךָ *let, I
pray, thy servant speak,* לֹא תִגְנֹב *thou shalt not steal,* הַיּוֹם
יוּמַת אֲדֹנִיָּהוּ *let Adonias die today,* מִי־יֹאמַר זִכִּיתִי לִבִּי *who
will say: I have purified my heart,* מִפְּרִי עֵץ הַגָּן נֹאכֵל *from
the fruit of the trees in the garden we may eat,* בַּיהוָֹה תִּתְהַלֵּל
נַפְשִׁי *may my soul exult in the Lord.*

§ 88. Use of the converted tenses.

1. The converted future (see § 27) may mean every
thing which, as explained above, can be signified by the
perfect It is to be observed, however, that such a form
is found only in the context of a continued speech, and
that, therefore, in the narrative the verb is first put in the
perfect and what follows in the converted future. Vav
in fact always retains a certain conjunctive power, whence
in this connection it is also called the consecutive Vav
Nevertheless the discourse begins often with the form וַיְהִי
and it came to pass, וַיֹּאמֶר *and he said,* because there is in
those cases some connection with the preceding book or
part of a book. Examples are: Gen. XXI, 1, וַיהוָֹה פָּקַד
אֶת־שָׂרָה כַּאֲשֶׁר אָמָר וַיַּעַשׂ יהוָֹה לְשָׂרָה כַּאֲשֶׁר דִּבֵּר *and the Lord
visited Sarah, as he had said, and the Lord did to Sarah, as
he had promised,* IV. Kings VIII, 1 וֶאֱלִישָׁע דִּבֶּר אֶל־הָאִשָּׁה
וַתָּקָם הָאִשָּׁה וַתַּעַשׂ כִּדְבַר אִישׁ הָאֱלֹהִים *and Eliseus spoke to
the woman, and the woman rose and did according to the word
of the man of God,* Judg II, 1 וַיַּעַל מַלְאַךְ־יהוָֹה מִן־הַגִּלְגָּל
אֶל־הַבֹּכִים *the angel of the Lord went up from Galgal to
Bochim.*

2. The **converted perfect** signifies all that is signified
by the future, and it has especially the power of the subjunctive and of the imperative. This form also occurs in a continued discourse only; but then it has fully the power of the
preceding future and imperative, v. g. וְהָיָה בַיּוֹם הַהוּא *and
it will come to pass on that day*, פֶּן־יָבוֹא וְהִכַּנִי *lest he come
and slay me*, אֶהְיֶה עִמָּךְ וְהִכִּיתָ אֶת־מִדְיָן *I shall be with thee,
and thou wilt defeat Madiam*, קַח לֹה וְאָסַפְתָּ *take and gather*.

§ 89. Paragogic or exhortative future.

The **first persons**, singular and plural, of the future,
amplified by הָ—ָ (paragogic, § 29) express an **exhortation**
of oneself to some action, v. g נַחְלְלָה *let us exult*; the form
also indicates a **request**, v g אֶעְבְּרָה בְאַרְצֶךְ *let me pass
through your land*; but where it is joined by the conjunction
ו with a preceding expression of a wish, it indicates a **deter-
mination** to do something, v g הָבִיאָה לִּי וְאֹכֵלָה *bring to
me, and I will eat*, וְאַבְלִיגָה מֵעַט יָשִׁית מִמֶּנִּי *let him leave me
that I may be refreshed a little*.

§ 90. Apocopated future.

The apocopated future is principally used, a) to command and forbid, v g יְהִי אוֹר *let there be light*, תּוֹצֵא
הָאָרֶץ נֶפֶשׁ חַיָּה *let the earth produce living souls*, אַל־יֵרֶא בִּפְלַגּוֹת
let him not see the streams, לֹא־תוֹרֵד שֵׂיבָתוֹ בְשָׁלֹם שְׁאֹל *thou
shalt not let his gray hairs go to hell (inferos) in peace*; it
is thus used especially after an imperative, v g הַעְתִּירוּ
אֶל־יְהוָֹה וְיָסֵר הַצְפַרְדְעִים *pray to the Lord that he will take
away the frogs*, סְקְלֻהוּ וִיָמֹת *stone him and let him die (to death)*,
b) in a **conditionate** sentence, v. g תִּגְזַר אֹמֶר וְיָקָם לָךְ *thou
wilt decree something and it will come (if thou ... it will
happen)*, and thus also לוּ יְהִי כִדְבָרֶךָ *may it be done according
to thy word!* c) commonly with the **conversive Vav**, v. g.
וַיָּמָת *and he died*, וַיִּגֶל *and he revealed*.

§ 91. Use of the imperative.

1. The imperative is used by the prophets in the sense of a most certain prediction, v. g בַּשָּׁנָה הַשְּׁלִישִׁית זִרְעוּ וְקִצְרוּ *in the third year you shall sow and reap,* יִתְפַּלֵּל בַּעַדְךָ וֶחְיֵה *he will pray for thee and thou shalt live,* צַהֲלִי קוֹלֵךְ *thou wilt neigh with thy voice*

2 When two forms of the imperative are joined together, the one is a condition or hypothesis, the following a consequent or apodosis, v. g עִזְבוּ פְתָאִים וִחְיוּ *if you give up foolishness, you shall live (give up .. and live)* זִרְעוּ לָכֶם לִצְדָקָה קִצְרוּ לְפִי חֶסֶד *if you sow in justice, you will reap in mercy.*

§ 92. Use of the infinitives, absolute and construct.

1 When an infinitive is used as the objective of another verb, it is either in the absolute or in the construct state, and it is placed either simply, or joined to לְ, v. g. לְמְדוּ הֵיטֵב *learn to do good,* לֹא אָבוּ הָלוֹךְ *they were not willing to go,* אָחֵל תֵּת *I begin to give,* לֹא יָדַעְתִּי דַבֵּר *I cannot speak,* לַמְּדֵנוּ לְהִתְפַּלֵּל *teach us how to pray,* וַיַּחְדְּלוּ לִבְנוֹת *they ceased to build*

2 The infinitive absolute, placed like a noun in an absolute case, is used adverbially, v. g. וָאָכֹת אֹתוֹ טָחוֹן הֵיטֵב *I broke him, crushing him entirely,* הַרְבֵּה יַעַבְדֶנּוּ *he will serve him much*

3 The Hebrew has a peculiar use of the infinitive absolute with the direct or personal form of the same verb When such an infinitive precedes the personal form, it lays more stress on the sense of the latter, v g. לֹא הַשְׁמֵיד אַשְׁמִיד *I shall not entirely destroy,* הֲמָלֹךְ תִּמְלֹךְ עָלֵינוּ *shalt thou truly reign over us?* But if the infinitive follows, it shows a continuation of the action, v. g אֹמְרִים אָמוֹר *continually saying,* וַיַּכֵּהוּ הָאִישׁ הַכֵּה וּפָצֹעַ *and the man was striking him frequently.*

4. The infinitive absolute, like the historical infinitive of the Romans, is used in Hebrew for a finite verb, whether the finite verb precedes or not, v. g. אַיֶּלֶת בַּשָּׂדֶה יָלְדָה וְעָזוֹב *the hind brought forth in the field and left it,* הַחַיּוֹת יָצוֹא וָשׁוֹב *the animals were going and coming*   Furthermore the infinitive absolute is used for the imperative, v g זָכוֹר אֶת־יוֹם הַשַּׁבָּת *remember the day of the Sabbath*

5. The infinitive construct may as a **verbal noun** fill any office in the phrase, and as such admits also of cases, suffixes and prepositions   Thus we read אֵין הָבִין *there is no understanding,* טוֹב לָנוּ שׁוּב *it is good for us to return* (nom.); עֵת סְפוֹד וְעֵת רְקוֹד *there is a time for weeping and a time for dancing* (gen); לֹא יָכְלוּ דַבֵּר *they could not speak* (acc.); נַחְבֵּאתָ לִבְרֹחַ *thou hast hidden in order to flee;* הִשָּׁמֶר לְךָ מְדַבֵּר *take care not to speak;* גַּם בִּשְׂחוֹק יִכְאַב־לֵב *even while laughing the heart is aching.*

6. The dative of the infinitive construct very frequently depends upon the verb substantive, and then expresses a possibility or a necessity, v. g הָיָה לָאֱכֹל *there was to eat,* אֵין לְרָאוֹת *it was not to be seen,* אֵין לָבוֹא *you cannot go in.*

7. The infinitive construct, like the finite verb, demands the complement of the verb; therefore, if the verb be transitive, it takes the accusative, v g לֹא אֹסִיף לְהָנִיד רֶגֶל יִשְׂרָאֵל *I will no more move the foot of Israel,* דַּבְּרוֹ *to speak with him,* לְהָרְגֵנִי *to kill me,* לָדַעַת אֹתִי *to know me,* לֹא טוֹב הוֹדִיעַ אֹתְךָ אֶת־כָּל־זֹאת *it is not good to acquaint you with all this,* לֹא חָפֵץ שָׁאַל בַּיהוָה *he would not interrogate the Lord.*

8. The **subject** of the **verb** is connected as a genitive with the infinitive construct, v g לֹא טוֹב הֱיוֹת הָאָדָם לְבַדּוֹ *it is not good for man (the being of man) to be alone,* כַּעֲבֹר סוּפָה וְאֵין רָשָׁע *like the passing of the storm, such is the wicked (and there is no wicked),* בְּצֵאת יִשְׂרָאֵל מִמִּצְרַיִם *in the going of Israel out of Egypt.*

Note   The suffix of the noun attached to the infinitive con-

struct expresses the subject, that of the verb the object, v g
לְחָרְגִי *that I may kill,* לְהָרְגֵנִי *that I may be killed.*

9. Where both the subject and the object accompany
the infinitive construct, the subject is placed nearer to the
verb, v. g. לִפְנֵי שַׁחֵת יהוה אֶת־סדם *before the Lord had de-*
stroyed Sodom, כַּהֲרִימִי קוֹלִי *while I am raising my voice,*
בִּשְׁלַח אֵלָיו הַמֶּלֶךְ צִדְקִיָּהוּ אֶת־פַּשְׁחוּר *when the king Sedecias*
sent to him Paschur.

§ 93. Use of the participle.

1. The participle may fill the place of the finite verb
in all tenses, v. g. נָהָר יֹצֵא, *a river was going out,* אֵהוּד מֵת
Ehud was dead, כַּחֲצֹת הַלַּיְלָה אֲנִי יֹצֵא *towards the middle of*
the night, I will go out It is most frequently used for the
present, and in a lively speech it has often הִנֵּה *(behold)*
before it, v g דוֹר הֹלֵךְ וְדוֹר בָּא *a generation cometh and a*
generation goeth, הִנְנִי גֹרֵשׁ אֶת־הָאֱמֹרִי מִפָּנֶיךָ *behold, I destroy*
the Amorrhite from before thee When the participle is combined
with הָיָה, it has the sense of the Latin imperfect or the
English compound tense, v. g מֹשֶׁה הָיָה רֹעֶה אֶת־צֹאן יִתְרוֹ
Moses was tending the flock of Jethro.

2. The complement of the verb is joined to the participle either in the same manner as to finite verbs, or else
it is placed in the genitive, v g הַיָּרֵא אֶת־דְּבַר יהוה *the*
one fearing the word of the Lord, לָבוּשׁ בַּדִּים *clad in linen,*
הָרֹדִים בָּעָם *those ruling the people,* קָמִים עָלַי *rising against*
me, יֹשֵׁב צִיּוֹן *dwelling in Sion,* שֹׁכְבֵי קָבֶר *lying in the grave,*
קָמַי *(those) rising against me* (see § 95).

Note Suffixes are joined to the participle with the same difference as when to the infinitive (§ 92, 8, note) v. g עֹשִׂי *creating*
me, עֹשִׂי *my creator* This distinction, however, hardly affects the sense

§ 94. Forms of the persons.

1. The indefinite subject (French: *on,* German: *man,*
English: *one, you, they, people* or *passive construction*) is expressed in Hebrew:

a) by the passive construction, v. g אָז הוּחַל לִקְרא *then they began to call;*

b) by the third person sing of the active, v. g אֶבֶן יָצוּק נְחוּשָׁה *by melting stone, (people) make copper;*

c) by the third plural of the active, v. g. לָהֶם יִקְרְאוּ חַוֹּת יָאִיר *they call them the huts of Jaïr;*

d) by the second person of the singular, v g לֹא־תָבוֹא שָׁמָּה *one shall not come there,* עַד בֹּאֲךָ *until one comes, you come.*

2. The third person masc of the perfect and of the future are often found used impersonally, v g. וַיְהִי *and it came to pass,* חָרָה לוֹ *he was incensed with anger (it burned to him),* לֹא יֻנַּח לָךְ *no rest will be given thee.* Thus likewise, we see sometimes the subject subjoined, v g. יְהִי מְאֹרֹת *let there be luminaries,* יָבוֹא הַשּׁוֹדְדִים *there come robbers (il vient des brigands).* More rarely is the third person femin. thus used impersonally, v g תַּמְטִיר *it rains,* עָשְׁקָה־לִּי *I feel anxious*

3. The masculine form of the pronouns is entirely preferred, and it is even used for the feminine, v. g. וַיֹּאמֶר אֵלֶיהָ עֲמֹד פֶּתַח *and he said to her: stand at the door,* שִׁמְעוּ פָּרוֹת הַבָּשָׁן *hear ye, cows of Basan.*

§ 95. Government of verbs.

1. Besides those verbs which from their nature appear transitive to us, the Hebrew employs many others as transitive and has them govern the accusative. Such are those which express the notion:

a) of sitting, dwelling, remaining,

b) going, coming, moving,

c) flowing, sprouting, teeming, dripping,

d) putting on, putting off,

e) abounding or wanting

2. There are other verbs transitively used in Hebrew,

which seem to us destitute of the transitive power not
so much from their nature and their sense as on account
of the common usage as עָנָה פְּלוֹנִי *he answered (to)
somebody* Finally others occur both with the transitive
and intransitive power, v g בָּכָה denotes both to *bewail
(somebody)* and *to shed tears*, שִׁיר to *sing* and *to celebrate in
song* These significations must be learned in the dictionary.
We add, however, a few constructions that appear singular
to us, as יֹשֵׁב אֹהֶל *dwelling in a tent (inhabiting a tent)*,
הֵם יָצְאוּ אֶת־הָעִיר *they went out of the city*, תִּירוֹשׁ יְקָבֶיךָ
יִפְרֹצוּ *thy garrets are full of wine* (see above *a, b, c*).

§ 96. Double accusative.

1 Causative conjugations of transitive verbs, according
to the nature of these verbs, admit a double accusative, viz
of the person and of the object, v g הִשְׁמִיעֲךָ אֶת־קוֹלוֹ *he
made thee hear his voice*, הָאֵל הַמְאַזְּרֵנִי חָיִל *God who has
girt me with strength.*

2 The verbs which have already in Kal a causative
sense (observe preceding §) take also in Kal a double
accusative, v. g וַיִּטָּעֵהוּ שֹׂרֵק *grant them to us*, חָנֵּנוּ אוֹתָם
and he planted it with selected vines, זְרָעָה אֲשֶׁר גִּמַּלְנוּ אֹתוֹ
the evil with which we afflicted him.

§ 97. Peculiar constructions of some verbs.

1. When one verb serves as a complement to another,
it is not always put in the infinitive, but sometimes in
the future, and this in the same person as the first, v g.
לֹא יָדַעְתִּי אֲכַנֶּה *I cannot flatter*, חָפֵץ יַגְדִּיל *he wanted to do
something great;* which idiom can be explained by supposing
אֲשֶׁר understood. Sometimes ו is inserted, v. g. וְשַׁבְתִּי אֲנִי
וָאֶרְאֶה *and I returned to see (I returned and I saw)* The
participle is likewise used as a complement, v g. אִישׁ יֹדֵעַ
מְנַגֵּן בְּכִנּוֹר *a man knowing how to play the Kinnor.*

7*

2. There are in the H. Scripture passages in which the notion of movement must be supplied between the verb and its object: חִלַּלְתָּ לָאָרֶץ נִזְרוֹ *thou hast defiled its crown (throwing it) to the earth,* הַחֲרִישׁוּ אֵלַי אִיִּים *be silent (while turned) to me, O islands!* This mode of expression is called pregnant construction.

§ 98. Conjunction of the subject with the predicate.

1. The *copula* is most frequently omitted, v g אֵלֶּה תוֹלְדוֹת *these are the generations (history),* גָּדוֹל יהוה *the Lord is great,* בְּתוֹרַת יהוה חֶפְצוֹ *in the law of the Lord is his pleasure.* Otherwise it is expressed by the personal pronoun of the 3 person, v g הַבְּהֵמָה אֲשֶׁר לֹא טְהֹרָה הִיא *the animals that are not clean* (see § 85, A, 1); should the subject be a pronoun and the predicate a participle, יֵשׁ and אֵין are used, v g אִם יֶשְׁךָ מוֹשִׁיעַ *if thou savest,* אֵינֶנּוּ מְבָרֵךְ *he does not bless.*

2. The predicate occasionally fails to agree in number and gender with its subject Thus collectives ordinarily take a plural predicate, v g. וַיִּקְרְאוּ בֵית־יִשְׂרָאֵל *the house of Israel cried,* יָרִיעוּ כָּל־הָעָם *let all the people shout,* רַבִּים עַם־הָאָרֶץ *the people of the land is numerous.* Likewise the majestic plural is, according to the sense, constructed with the singular, v. g בְּעָלָיו יוּמָת *let his master die,* קָשֶׁה אֲדֹנִים *the master is hard* Moreover, the plural nouns of animals and of inanimate things are sometimes used with the singular femin., v. g. שְׁאַל־נָא בְהֵמוֹת וְתוֹדֶךָּ *interrogate the animals, and they will inform thee,* לֹא תִמְעַד אֲשֻׁרָיו *his steps will not fail.*

3. If the subject is joined with a genitive, the predicate sometimes agrees in gender and number with the latter, because the genitive appears to be the weightier part of a composite notion, v. g עֵינֵי גַבְהוּת אָדָם שָׁפֵל *the conceited eyes*

of man have been humbled, קוֹל־נְגִידִים נֶחְבָּאוּ *the voice of the chiefs became mute.*

C Syntax of the particles.

§ 99. Syntax of the adverbs.

1 The adverbs of negation לֹא and אַל are different in this, that לֹא (*non*) declares, אַל (*ne*) forbids, v. g. לֹא יֵלֵךְ *he will not go,* אַל־יֵלֵךְ *he shall not go;* but לֹא is also used as a particle of severe prohibition, as in לֹא תִגְנֹב *thou shalt not steal.*

2 A double negation does not affirm as in Latin and English, but is a stronger negation as in Greek, v. g. אֵין כָּסֶף לֹא נֶחְשָׁב *silver will be counted as nothing.*

3. The word לֹא is also used as an answer for *no.* There is no corresponding word of affirmation for *yes,* but to express it, the word is repeated as it is often in Latin, v. g. הֲיֵשׁ דָּבָר מֵאֵת יְהֹוָה וַיֹּאמֶר יֵשׁ *is there a word from the Lord? and he said: there is.*

§ 100. Syntax of the prepositions.

The Hebrew has this peculiarity that it combines various prepositions into one; thus the prepositions which indicate motion are placed before the prepositions which designate the place, in order to signify the change of local conditions which existed before or begin to exist now; v. g. מֵעַל *from over,* מֵאַחַר *from behind,* מִתַּחַת *from under,* מֵעִם *from with,* also אֶל אַחֲרֵי מֵאֵת *to, after (something),* מְחוּץ לְ *from outside, outside (something),* אֶל מחוּץ לְ *to, outside (something),* etc.

§ 101. Syntax of the conjunctions.

Frequently a part of compound conjunctions is omitted; thus, v. g. for יַעַן אֲשֶׁר, either יַעַן alone is written, or אֲשֶׁר, v. g. יַעַן וּבְיַעַן הִטְעוּ אֶת־עַמִּי *because they deceived my people* (cf § 85, D 4) In an emphatic discourse sometimes the conjunction is entirely omitted and is compensated by a grave accent; this happens especially in conditional and comparative sentences, v. g אֹכְלֵי עַמִּי אָכְלוּ לָחֶם *(eating my people they eat bread) they eat my people like bread,* חָטָאתִי מָה אֶפְעַל לָךְ *if I sin, what do I do to you?*

EXERCISES.

First instruction in reading.

v°thôrath	la'adham	ner	Yhvh	Mitsvath
² וְתוֹרַת	¹ לָאָדָם	נֵר	יְהוָֹה	מִצְוַת
and the law,	to man,	is a lamp,	of the Lord,	The precept,

		laddarech	'ôr	'elohîm
		³ לַדָּרֶךְ׃	אוֹר	אֱלֹהִים
		for the way.	is a light,	of God,

úbh°racha	me'olam	Shadday	Chesedh
⁵ וּבְרָכָה	⁴ מֵעוֹלָם	שַׁדַּי	חֶסֶד
and a blessing,	is from eternity,	of the Almighty,	The mercy,

	vadhôr	l°dhôr	l°tsaddîk
	⁷ וָדוֹר׃	לְדוֹר	⁶ לַצַּדִּיק
	and generation.	in generation,	is to the just (man),

l°sachal	hassımcha	bîmê	hayyayın	Mokesh
לְסָכָל	הַשִּׂמְחָה	⁸ בִּימֵי	הַיַּיִן	מוֹקֵשׁ
to the fool,	of joy,	in the days,	is (the) wine,	A snare,

		l°chacham	vegham
		לֶחָכָם׃	וְגַם
		to the wise (man).	and also,

úma	Yisra'el	c(h)elohê	gadhôl	'el	Mi
¹⁰ וּמָה	יִשְׂרָאֵל	⁹ כֵּאלֹהֵי	גָּדוֹל	אֵל	מִי
and what,	of Israël,	like the God,	great,	ıs a God,	Who,

	ha'addîr	be'ênê	ha'°nôsh
	הָאַדִּיר׃	בְּעֵינֵי	הָאֱנוֹשׁ
	of the all-powerful.	ın the eyes,	ıs man,

’Adhonay	ha’abh	lᵉyathôm	vᵉhû	yᵉshû‘ath
אֲדוֹנָי	הָאָב	לְיָתוֹם	וְהוּא	יְשׁוּעַת
The Lord,	is the father,	to the orphan,	and he is,	the salvation,

ha’ebhyônîm
הָאֶבְיוֹנִים׃
of the poor

’én	zecher	lacc(h)ᵉsîl	‘im-hachᵃchamîm
אֵין	זֵכֶר	לַכְּסִיל	עִם־הַחֲכָמִים
(There is) no,	remembrance,	of the fool,	with the wise,

lᵉ‘olam	shem	hassachal	c(h)ᵉ‘ashan
לְעוֹלָם	שֵׁם	הַסָּכָל	כֶּעָשָׁן׃
for ever,	the name,	of the unwise,	is like smoke.

Hammishpat	ladhonay	basshamayim	ûmeha’ᵉlohim
הַמִּשְׁפָּט	¹¹לַאדֹנָי	¹²בַּשָּׁמַיִם	¹³וּמֵהָאֱלֹ׳חִים
The judgment,	is to the Lord,	in the heavens,	and from God,

col-hasshillem
כָּל־הַשָּׁלֵּם׃
is all retribution.

Dibhrê	hechacham	masc(h)îlîm	bᵉchol-ha’emer
¹⁴דִבְרֵי	הֶחָכָם	מַשְׂכִּילִים	בְּכָל־הָאָמֶר
The words,	of the wise man,	are prudent,	in every saying,

‘im	ha’îsh	hayyashar	marpê	lashôn
עִם	הָאִישׁ	הַיָּשָׁר	מַרְפֵּא	לָשׁוֹן׃
with,	the man,	the right (one),	there is meekness,	of the tongue.

Shochadh	haresha‘	mokesh	lᵉshophet
שֹׁחַד	הָרָשָׁע	מוֹקֵשׁ	לְשֹׁפֵט
The present,	of the wicked (man),	is a snare,	to the judge,

’îsh	mattan	massha’ôn	lᵉtsedhek
אִישׁ	מַתָּן	מַשָּׂאוֹן	לְצֶדֶק׃
a man,	of gift,	(is) a fraud,	to justice.

cherebh	ha'ᵉlohîm	bᵉyadh	hattsaddîk	Tᵉshûʻath
חֶרֶב	הָאֱלֹהִים	בְּיַד	הַצַּדִּיק	תְּשׁוּעַת
sword,	of God,	is in the hand,	of the just man,	The salvation,

	l'ʼish-chamas		c(h)ôach	vᵉkesheth
	לְאִישׁ־חָמָס׃		כֹּחַ	וְקֶשֶׁת
	to the man, of violence.		are the strength,	and bow,

tochachath	ûmeʻᵃdhonay	hasshophet	Yhvh
תּוֹכַחַת	וּמֵאֲדֹנָי	הַשֹּׁפֵט	יהֹוָה
is (the) retribution,	and from the Lord,	is the judge,	The Lord,

	tebhel	col-yoshᵉbhê	
	תֵּבֵל׃	כָּל־יֹשְׁבֵי	
	of the globe.	of all the inhabitants,	

The "copula" (verb substantive), which is omitted in Hebrew, is to be supplied everywhere

1 3. Sign of dat with the article; 2. Vav conjunctive; 4 Prepos. מִן; 5. Vav conjunct ; 6 Sign of dat ; 7 Vav conjunct ; 8. Prepos. בְּ and plur noun ירם irregular; 9. Prepos כְּ; 10 Vav conjunct ; 11. Sign of dat ; 12. Prepos. ב with the article; 13 Vav conjunct , prepos. מִן and art ; 14. Constr state, plur.

Nouns, regular verbs, guttural verbs.

I.

חַנּוּן ¹וְרַחוּם ²הָאֱלֹהִים אֲשֶׁר ³הִמְשִׁיל דָּוִד ⁴בְּיִשְׂרָאֵל׃ יְהוֹשֻׁעַ כָּרַת כָּל־יְרִיחוֹ ⁵מֵאָדָם עַד־בְּהֵמָה ⁶וַיִּקְטֹל כָּל־⁷יֹשְׁבֵי ⁸הָעִיר ⁹מֵאִישׁ וְעַד־אִשָּׁה ⁹מִנַּעַר וְעַד־זָקֵן ⁹מִשּׁוֹר וְעַד־הַחֲמוֹר׃ ¹⁰זָכֹר אֶת־יְהֹוָה ¹⁰יִדְרֹשׁ אֶת־אֱלֹהֵי הַשָּׁמַיִם וְהָאָרֶץ ¹¹בַּבַּיִת ¹²וּבַדֶּרֶךְ יוֹם וָיוֹם׃ הַיּוֹם ¹³הַשְּׁבִיעִי שָׁבַת כָּל־הָעָם ¹⁴לַיהֹוָה בַּפַּחְנָה׃ בְּיוֹם מִשְׁפָּט ¹⁵יַבְדִּיל יְהֹוָה אֵת הַצַּדִּיקִים מִן הַחַטָּאִים׃ דָּרַךְ הָרְשָׁעִים ¹⁶כַּצַּלְמָוֶת וְקֵץ הַצַּדִּיקִים ¹⁶כַּשַּׁחַר׃ יְהֹוָה ¹⁷נָתַן ¹⁷לָאָדָם אֶת־גַּן עֵדֶן ¹⁸לִשְׁמֹר׃ ¹⁹נֹתֵן הָאֱלֹהִים ²⁰לִבְנֵי אָדָם פְּרִי הָאָרֶץ׃

1. ו conjunctive. 2. Artic. and subst. 3. Hiphil 4. ב and subst. 5 מִן and subst. 6. Fut. conv Hiphil 7. Partic 8 Artic. and subst. 9. 9. 9 מִן and subst 10. 10. Imperativ. 11. ב, artic and subst. 12 ו, ב, artic and subst 13. Ordinal. 14 Dativ. 15. Fut Hiph. 16. 16 כ and subst. 17. Dativ artic. 18 Dativ infinitive 19 Particip. 20 Dativ constr stat plur (בֶּן son)

II.

¹הָאִישׁ אֲשֶׁר לֹא הָלַךְ ²בַּעֲצַת רְשָׁעִים ³וּבְדֶרֶךְ חַטָּאִים
לֹא עָמָד: כָּל־⁴הַדָּבָר חַזֶּה ⁵נִכְתַּב עַל סֵפֶר ⁶הַמְּלָכִים ⁷לִיהוּדָה:
⁸בְּרֵאשִׁית בָּרָא אֱלֹהִים אֵת הַשָּׁמַיִם וְאֵת הָאָרֶץ: ⁹וַיַּבְדֵּל אֱלֹהִים
בֵּין הָאוֹר ¹⁰וּבֵין הַחֹשֶׁךְ: ¹¹וַיְבָרֶךְ יְהוָה אֶת־יּוֹם ¹²הַשְּׁבִיעִי
¹³וַיְקַדֵּשׁ ¹⁴אֹתוֹ: כֹּה כָתוֹב בְּיַד הַנָּבִיא ¹⁵שָׂמַח הַיַּיִן לְבַב־אֱנוֹשׁ:
¹⁶וַיְשַׁלַּח יְהוָה אֱלֹהִים אֶת־הָאָדָם ¹⁷מִגַּן עֵדֶן ¹⁸לַעֲבֹד אֶת הָאֲדָמָה
אֲשֶׁר לָקַח־²⁰מִשָּׁם:

1 Artic and subst 2. ב and constr stat 3 ו, ב, subst 4 Artic and subst 5 Niphal 6 Artic and subst. plur. 7 Dativ. 8 ב
and subst 9 Fut convers Hiph. 10 ו and subst 11 Fut convers
Piél 12 Ordinal 13. Fut convers Piel. 14 Accus pers. pronoun.
s. § 74 15 Piël 16 Fut Piël 17 מן and גַּן. 18 Dativ infinitiv
19 Pual 20 מן and שָׁם.

III.

¹בַּמִּדְבָּר אָמְרוּ ²בְנֵי יִשְׂרָאֵל זָכַרְנוּ אֶת־הַדָּגָה אֲשֶׁר אָכַלְנוּ
בְמִצְרַיִם חִנָּם: ³וַיִּקְרָא יְהוָה אֶל־מֹשֶׁה כֹּה ⁴תְדַבֵּר ⁵לְבֵית יַעֲקֹב
⁶לִבְנֵי יִשְׂרָאֵל: וְלֹא שָׁמַע הַמֶּלֶךְ אֶל־הָעָם וַיִּשְׁלְחוּ וַיִּקְרְאוּ אֶת־
*יָרָבְעָם ⁷וַיַּמְלִיכוּ אֹת יָרָבְעָם עַל־כָּל־יִשְׂרָאֵל: וְעַתָּה יִשְׂרָאֵל ⁸שְׁמַע
אֶל־⁹הַחֻקִּים וְאֶל־הַמִּשְׁפָּטִים אֲשֶׁר אָנֹכִי ¹⁰מְלַמֵּד אֶת הָעָם: ¹¹וַיְדַבֵּר
יְהוָה אֶל־כָּל־יִשְׂרָאֵל בְּחֹרֵב מִתּוֹךְ הָאֵשׁ קוֹל דְּבָרִים אַתֶּם ¹²שֹׁמְעִים:

1. ב, Artic and subst. 2. Constr stat pl s בֶּן 3 Fut. convers
4 2 pers. fut Piël. 5 Dativ 6. Dativ. plur. constr stat 7 Fut
Hiph *Prop noun 8. Imp. 9 Plur v. חק. 10. Particip Piël. 11. Fut.
conv. Piël 12 Particip. Kal. in plur

IV.

¹אֱהַב אֵת יְהוָה אֱלֹהֵי הַשָּׁמַיִם וְהָאָרֶץ וּשְׁמַרְתָּ אֶת הַחֻקִּים
וְאֵת הַמִּשְׁפָּטִים כָּל־²הַיָּמִים: ³שִׁמְעוּ־זֹאת כָּל־הָעַמִּים ⁴הַאֲזִינוּ כָּל־
⁵יֹשְׁבֵי הָאָרֶץ: וַיִּשְׁמַע יְהוָה אֱלֹהִים אֶל־קוֹל הַנַּעַר וַיִּקְרָא מַלְאַךְ
אֱלֹהִים אֶל־⁶הָגָר מִן־הַשָּׁמָיִם: אַל־⁷תִּירְאִי כִּי־שָׁמַע אֱלֹהִים אֶל־קוֹל
הַנָּעַר: וַיֹּאמֶר ⁸שָׁאוּל אֶל־⁹שְׁמוּאֵל חָטָאתִי כִּי עָבַרְתִּי אֶת־פִּי־

יהֹוָֽה וְאֶת־ דִּבְרֵי שְׁמוּאֵל כִּי יָרֵאתִי אֶת־הָעָם ¹⁰וָאֶשְׁמַע בְּקוֹל
הָעָם הַזֶּה: וְזֹאת אוֹת בְּרִית אֲשֶׁר אֲנִי ¹¹נֹתֵן לָאָרֶץ אֶת־קַשְׁתִּי
¹²נָתַתִּי ¹³בֶּעָנָן לְאוֹת בְּרִית עוֹלָֽם:

1 Imperat (s. § 33)   2 Plur s יוֹם   3 Imperat plur   4. Imperat. Hiph plur   5 Partic Kal plur   6 Hagar propr noun   7 Fut
2 p fem (s יָרֵא he feared)   8 Saul   9 Samuel   10 Fut conv. Kal
1 pers   11. Partic   12 נָתַן.   13 בְ with artic הָ.

V.

יֹשֵׁב שָׁמַיִם יְהֹוָה מֶלֶךְ וַיִּמְלֹךְ בָּאָֽרֶץ: אֲדֹנָי יִשְׁפֹּט הַתֵּבֵל
בְּצֶֽדֶק: אִם יְהֹוָה לֹא יִשְׁמֹר עִיר שָׁוְא שָׁקַד שֹׁמֵר: מִי יִסַפֵּר
אֶת־כּוֹכְבֵי הַשָּׁמָיִם: זַמְּרוּ לַיהֹוָה כָּל־צַדִּיקִים בָּאָֽרֶץ: × נִסְמַכְתָּ
בֶּאֱמֶת הָאֲנָשִׁים הָאֵלֶּה וַתִּמָּכֵר בְּיַד אֹיְבִים: נִבְחָר הַדַּעַת וְהַחָכְמָה
מִכֶּסֶף וּמִזָּהָב: יְהֹוָה שֹׂנֵא אִישׁ מְתַכַבֵּד וְאֹהֵב אֶבְיוֹנִים וְצַדִּיקִים:
טוֹב לָאִישׁ אֲשֶׁר הָלַךְ בְּדֶרֶךְ מוּסַר שַׁדַּי וִישְׁתַּמֵּר מֵעָוֹן:

VI.

עֲצַת חֲכָמִים תַּעֲמֹד לְעוֹלָם וּמַחְשְׁבוֹת הַצַּדִּיקִים לֹא תַחָשַׁכְנָה
לְדֹר וָדֹר: וַיַּעֲבֹרוּ הַלְוִיִּם וַיַּעֲמִידוּ אֶת אֲרוֹן הַבְּרִית אֶל הַמָּקוֹם
בָּאֹֽהֶל: אִם תַּעַמְדוּ לִפְנֵי אוֹיְבִים לַמִּלְחָמָה אַל־תַּחְפְּזוּ וְאַל־
תַּעַרְצוּ מִפְּנֵי־הָחָרֶב: תָּחֵנָּךְ אֶת הַשָּׂנֵא בָּאָבֵל וְאַל־תַּאֲמִין בְּחֶסֶד
אֹיְבִים: שַׁדַּי אַתָּה יְהֹוָה הֶעֱמַקְתָּ לְהַסְתִּיר אֹרְחוֹת הַמִּשְׁפָּט: נֶאֱמָן
מוּסַר הָאֹהֵב וְנַעְתָּרוֹת שָׁוְא נְשִׁיקוֹת הַשָּׂנֵא: לֹא הֶאֱמִין הָעָם
בַּיהֹוָֽה וַיַּעַבְדוּ בְּנֵי יִשְׂרָאֵל אֶת אֱלֹהִים אֲחֵרִים:

VII.

אַל־תִּבָּהֵל בְּרוּחַ לִכְעֹס כִּי כַעַס בְּחֵק כְּסִילִים יַעֲמֹד: בָּהֵל
הָאִישׁ הַהוּא עַל־הַלָּשׁוֹן וַיְמַהֵר וַיְדַבֵּר בִּדְבָרִים רַבִּים: אַתָּה
יְהֹוָה בֵּרַכְתָּ אֶת הָעָם וּמְבֹרָךְ שֵׁם הָאֱלֹהִים לְעוֹלָם: אִישׁ דָּמִים
וּמִרְמָה יְתָעֵב שַׁדַּי וְלֵצִים נֹפְלִים מַהֵר בְּדַרְכָּם יִמָּחֲצוּ: מָהֲרוּ הַבָּנוֹת
וְדָרְשׁוּ אֶת הַיֶּלֶד אֲשֶׁר בָּרַח בִּירֵאַת הָרֹדְפִים: גַּם הַזְּקֵנִים וּמוֹעֲדֵי
רָגֶל לֹא מָצְאוּ חֶסֶד בְּעֵינֵי הָאֹיְבִים: יֶאֱהַב אֲדֹנָי אֶת אֹהֲבֵי הַיֹּשֶׁר
כְּרַחֵם אָב אֶת־הַבָּנִים יְרַחֵם יְהֹוָה אֶת־הַצַּדִּיקִים:

Irregular verbs and suffixes.

VIII.

¹יָשׁוּב עָפָר אֶל הָאָרֶץ וְהָרוּחַ תָּשׁוּב אֶל־הָאֱלֹהִים: ²הוֹצִיא הָאֱלֹהִים אֶת־בְּנֵי יִשְׂרָאֵל מֵאֶרֶץ מִצְרַיִם: ²וַיֵּצְאוּ אַנְשֵׁי הָעִיר לִקְרַאת יִשְׂרָאֵל לַמִּלְחָמָה ³וַיָּנֻסוּ כָל־יִשְׂרָאֵל דֶּרֶךְ הַמִּדְבָּר: וַיֹּאמֶר יְהוָֹה אֶל־הָאָדָם ⁴הֲמִן־הָעֵץ אֲשֶׁר ⁵צִוִּיתִיךָ לְבִלְתִּי ⁶אֲכָל־מִמֶּנּוּ אָכָלְתָּ: ⁷וַיֹּאמֶר הָאָדָם הָאִשָּׁה נָתְנָה־לִּי מִן־הָעֵץ וָאֹכֵל: וַיֹּאמֶר יְהוָֹה אֶל אַבְרָם הִנֵּה ⁹בְרִיתִי אִתָּךְ ¹⁰וְהָיִיתָ לְאַב הֲמוֹן גּוֹיִם: ¹¹בְּנִי ¹¹תּוֹרָתִי אַל־תִּשְׁכַּח וּמִצְוֹתַי ¹²יִצֹּר לִבֶּךָ: חֶסֶד וֶאֱמֶת אַל־יַעַזְבֻךָ ¹³קָשְׁרֵם עַל־נַרְגְּרֹתֶיךָ כָּתְבֵם עַל־לוּחַ לִבֶּךָ: ¹⁴בְּטַח אֶל־יְהוָֹה בְּכָל־לִבֶּךָ וְאֶל־בִּינָתְךָ אַל־¹⁵תִּשָּׁעֵן: בְּכָל־דְּרָכֶיךָ ¹⁶דָעֵהוּ וְהוּא יְיַשֵּׁר אֹרְחֹתֶיךָ: אַל־¹⁷תְּהִי חָכָם בְּעֵינֶיךָ ¹⁸יְרָא אֶת־יְהוָֹה ¹⁹וְסוּר ²⁰מֵרָע: אַל־תֹּאמַר לְרֵעֲךָ ²¹לֵךְ וָשׁוּב ²²וּמָחָר ²³אֶתֵּן ²³אָתָּן אִתָּךְ:

1. Verb ע״ו.   2. 2. פ״א.   3 ע״ו   4. ה interrogative.   5. לֹ״ה Piël.
6. Inf constr.   7 פ״א.   8 פ״א   9 Subst with suffix   10 לֹ״ה
11. 11. Subst. with suffix.   12. פ״ן   13 Imperat with suffix.   14. Imperat   15. Fut Niph   16. פ״ה imperat with suffix.   17. חָיָה.   18 Imperat   19. ע״ו.   20. מן.   21. Imperat פ״ו   22. פ״ן.   23. ר s. § 75

א   חַכְמֵי הַקֶּדֶם:

1 ¹וַיְהִי כַּאֲשֶׁר ²נוֹלַד ³יֵשׁוּעַ ⁴בְּבֵית־לֶחֶם יְהוּדָה ⁵בִּימֵי ⁶חוֹרוֹדוֹס הַמֶּלֶךְ הִנֵּה ⁷חַכָמִים ⁷בָּאוּ מִקֶּדֶם ⁸יְרוּשָׁלַיְמָה: 2 ⁹וַיֹּאמְרוּ אַיֵּה מֶלֶךְ־הַיְּהוּדִים ¹⁰הַנּוֹלָד כִּי ¹¹רָאִינוּ כוֹכָבוֹ בַּקֶּדֶם ¹²וַנָּבֹא ¹³לְהִשְׁתַּחֲוֹת לוֹ: 3 וַיִּשְׁמַע חוֹרוֹדוֹס הַמֶּלֶךְ וַיִּרְגַּז הוּא וְכָל־יְרוּשָׁלָיִם עִמּוֹ: 4 וַיַּקְהֵל אֶת־כָּל־¹⁴רָאשֵׁי הַכֹּהֲנִים ¹⁵וְהַסּוֹפְרִים בָּעָם וַיִּשְׁאַל אֹתָם אַיֵּה ¹⁶יִוָּלֵד ¹⁷הַמָּשִׁיחַ: 5 וַיֹּאמְרוּ אֵלָיו בְּבֵית־לֶחֶם יְהוּדָה כִּי כֹה־כָּתוּב בְּיַד הַנָּבִיא: 6 וְאַתָּה בֵּית־לֶחֶם אֶרֶץ יְהוּדָה ¹⁸אֵינֵךְ צָעִיר ¹⁹בְּאַלְפֵי יְהוּדָה מִמֵּךְ יֵצֵא מֹשֵׁל אֲשֶׁר יִרְעֶה אֶת־עַמִּי יִשְׂרָאֵל: 7 אָז קָרָא חוֹרוֹדוֹס לְחַכְמֵי הַקֶּדֶם בַּסֵּתֶר וַיַּחְקֹר מֵהֶם אֶת־הָעֵת אֲשֶׁר ²⁰נִרְאָה ²¹בָהּ הַכּוֹכָב: 8 וַיִּשְׁלַח אֹתָם

לְבֵית־לָחֶם וַיֹּאמֶר ²²לְכוּ וְדִרְשׁוּ הֵיטֵב עַל־הַיֶּלֶד וְכַאֲשֶׁר תִּמְצָאוּהוּ
²³הֲשִׁיבוּנִי דָבָר לְמַעַן ²⁴אֵלֵךְ גַּם־אָנֹכִי ²⁵לְהִשְׁתַּחֲוֹת לוֹ׃ 9 וְכַאֲשֶׁר
שָׁמְעוּ אֶת־הַמֶּלֶךְ וַיֵּלֵכוּ וְהִנֵּה הַכּוֹכָב אֲשֶׁר ²⁶רָאוּ בַּקֶּדֶם הָלַךְ
לִפְנֵיהֶם עַד אֲשֶׁר־בָּא וַיַּעֲמֹד מִמַּעַל ²⁷לַאֲשֶׁר הָיָה שָׁם הַיֶּלֶד׃
10 ²⁸וְכִרְאוֹתָם אֶת־הַכּוֹכָב שָׂמְחוּ שִׂמְחָה גְדוֹלָה עַד־מְאֹד׃
11 ²⁹וּבְבֹאָם ³⁰הַבַּיְתָה מָצְאוּ אֶת־הַיֶּלֶד עִם ³¹מִרְיָם אִמּוֹ ³²וַיִּפְּלוּ
אַרְצָה ³³וַיִּשְׁתַּחֲווּ לוֹ ³⁴וּבְפִתְחָם אוֹצְרוֹתֵיהֶם ³⁵הִקְרִיבוּ לוֹ
מִנְחוֹת אֶת־זָהָב וְאֶת־לְבוֹנָה וְאֶת־מֹר׃ 12 וְהֵם נִזְהֲרוּ מֵאֱלֹהִים
בַּחֲלוֹם לְבִלְתִּי שׁוּב אֶל־הוֹרוֹדוֹס וַיֵּלְכוּ בְדֶרֶךְ אַחֵר לְאַרְצָם׃
13 וַיְהִי ³⁶בְּלֶכְתָּם וְהִנֵּה מַלְאַךְ יְהֹוָה נִרְאָה לְיוֹסֵף בַּחֲלוֹם ³⁷לֵאמֹר׃
14 קוּם ³⁸קַח אֶת־הַיֶּלֶד וְאֶת־אִמּוֹ וּבְרַח מִצְרַיְמָה וֶהְיֵה שָׁם עַד־
אֲשֶׁר אֹמַר אֵלֶיךָ כִּי יְבַקֵּשׁ הוֹרוֹדוֹס אֶת־הַיֶּלֶד ³⁹לְאַבְּדוֹ׃ 15 ⁴⁰וַיָּקָם
⁴¹וַיִּקַּח אֶת־הַיֶּלֶד וְאֶת־אִמּוֹ בַּלַּיְלָה וַיֵּלֶךְ מִצְרָיְמָה׃ 16 וַיְהִי שָׁם
עַד־מוֹת הוֹרוֹדוֹס ⁴²לְקַיֵּם הַנֶּאֱמָר עַל־פִּי יְהֹוָה בְּיַד הַנָּבִיא לֵאמֹר
מִמִּצְרַיִם קָרָאתִי לִבְנִי׃ 17 וַיְהִי ⁴³כִּרְאוֹת הוֹרוֹדוֹס כִּי ⁴⁴הֵתֵלוּ
בוֹ חַכְמֵי הַקֶּדֶם וַיִּקְצֹף עַד־מְאֹד׃ 18 ⁴⁵וַיִּשְׁלַח ⁴⁵וַיַּךְ אֶת־כָּל־הַיְלָדִים
אֲשֶׁר בְּבֵית־לָחֶם וּבְכָל־גְּבוּלֶיהָ מִבֶּן־שְׁנָתַיִם וּלְמַטָּה כְּפִי הָעֵת אֲשֶׁר
חָקַר מֵחַכְמֵי הַקֶּדֶם׃ 19 אָז ⁴⁶הִתְקַיֵּם הַנֶּאֱמָר בְּיַד יִרְמְיָהוּ הַנָּבִיא
לֵאמֹר׃ 20 קוֹל בְּרָמָה נִשְׁמָע נְהִי בְכִי תַמְרוּרִים רָחֵל ⁴⁷מְבַכָּה
עַל־בָּנֶיהָ ⁴⁸מֵאֲנָה לְהִנָּחֵם כִּי ⁴⁹אֵינֶנּוּ׃ 21 וַיְהִי אַחֲרֵי מוֹת
הוֹרוֹדוֹס וְהִנֵּה מַלְאַךְ יְהֹוָה נִרְאָה בַּחֲלוֹם לְיוֹסֵף בְּמִצְרַיִם לֵאמֹר׃
22 קוּם ⁵⁰קַח אֶת־הַיֶּלֶד וְאֶת־אִמּוֹ ⁵¹וְלֵךְ אֶל־אֶרֶץ יִשְׂרָאֵל כִּי ⁵²מֵתוּ
הַמְבַקְשִׁים אֶת־נֶפֶשׁ הַיֶּלֶד׃ 23 וַיָּקָם וַיִּקַּח אֶת־הַיֶּלֶד וְאֶת־אִמּוֹ
וַיָּבֹא אֶל־אֶרֶץ יִשְׂרָאֵל׃ 24 ⁵³וּבְשָׁמְעוֹ כִּי מָלַךְ אַרְקְלָאוֹס בִּיהוּדָה
תַּחַת הוֹרוֹדוֹס אָבִיו וַיִּירָא ⁵⁴לָלֶכֶת שָׁמָּה׃ 25 וַיְהִי כִּי נִזְהַר
מֵאֱלֹהִים בַּחֲלוֹם וַיֵּלֶךְ אֶל־⁵⁵גְּלִילוֹת הַגָּלִיל׃ 26 וַיָּבֹא וַיֵּשֶׁב בְּעִיר
אֲשֶׁר שְׁמָהּ נָצָרֶת׃

1 Fut apoc. verb הָיָה. 2 Niph v. יָלַד 3 Jesus 4. Bethlehem.
5 ב plural 6 יום Herod 7 בוא 8 Local ה. 9. אָמַר fut
10 Partic. Niph (יָלַד) 11 רָאָה 12 בוא 13 שָׁחָה Hithpalel (§ 44,
not 2) 14. ראש. 15 The scribes. 16. Fut Niph v. יָלַד. 17. The
Messiah 18 s § 72 19 אֶלֶף M men, a tribe, here a great city.

20 Niph. v רָאָה 21 אֲשֶׁר בָּהּ s § 85 D 22 Imp v. יָלַךְ
23 Imp Hiph v שׁוּב with suff 24 Fut v יָלַךְ 1. pers 25. שָׁחָה
(s 13) 26 רָאָה. 27 joined with שָׁם 28 Inf v רָאָה with suff
and prepos 29 Inf v בּוֹא with suff and prepos 30 ח paragogic 31 Mary 32 נָפַל 33 Vd 13 34 Inf. v פָּתַח (vd 28).
35 Hiphil 36 Inf v יָלַךְ (vd 28) 37 s § 17 2c 38 Imp v.
לָקַח 39 Inf Piel, אָבַד 40 קוּם 41 לָקַח 42 Inf Piel v. קוּם
(Ezech 13 6) 43 Inf v רָאָה 44 Piel v הֵחַל 45 Fut apoc Hiph
v נָכָה 46 Hithpaèl (vd 42) 47 Part Piél fem. 48 3 fem Piel
v צָאַן 49 s § 72 50 Imp v לָקַח 51 Imp. v. יָלַךְ 52. מוּת
53 Inf v שָׁמַע (vd 28). 54 Inf v יָלַךְ dativ. 55. Galilee.

ב :אַבְרָהָם

1 וְהָאֱלֹהִים נִסָּה אֶת־אַבְרָהָם וַיֹּאמֶר אֵלָיו אַבְרָהָם וַיֹּאמֶר
הִנֵּנִי׃ 2 וַיֹּאמֶר [1]קַח־נָא אֶת־בִּנְךָ אֶת־יְחִידְךָ אֲשֶׁר־אָהַבְתָּ אֶת־
יִצְחָק [2]וְלֶךְ־לְךָ אֶל־אֶרֶץ הַמֹּרִיָּה [3]וְהַעֲלֵהוּ שָׁם לְעֹלָה עַל אַחַד
הֶהָרִים אֲשֶׁר אֹמַר אֵלֶיךָ׃ 3 וַיַּשְׁכֵּם אַבְרָהָם בַּבֹּקֶר וַיַּחֲבֹשׁ אֶת־
חֲמֹרוֹ וַיִּקַּח אֶת־שְׁנֵי נְעָרָיו אִתּוֹ וְאֵת יִצְחָק בְּנוֹ וַיְבַקַּע עֲצֵי עֹלָה
[4]וַיָּקָם וַיֵּלֶךְ אֶל־הַמָּקוֹם אֲשֶׁר אָמַר־לוֹ הָאֱלֹהִים׃ 4 בַּיּוֹם הַשְּׁלִישִׁי
[5]וַיִּשָּׂא אַבְרָהָם אֶת־עֵינָיו [6]וַיַּרְא אֶת־הַמָּקוֹם מֵרָחֹק׃ 5 וַיֹּאמֶר
אַבְרָהָם אֶל־נְעָרָיו [7]שְׁבוּ־לָכֶם פֹּה עִם־הַחֲמוֹר וַאֲנִי וְהַנַּעַר [8]נֵלְכָה
עַד־כֹּה וְנִשְׁתַּחֲוֶה וְנָשׁוּבָה אֲלֵיכֶם׃ 6 וַיִּקַּח אַבְרָהָם אֶת־עֲצֵי הָעֹלָה
[9]וַיָּשֶׂם עַל־יִצְחָק בְּנוֹ וַיִּקַּח בְּיָדוֹ אֶת־הָאֵשׁ וְאֶת־הַמַּאֲכֶלֶת וַיֵּלְכוּ
שְׁנֵיהֶם יַחְדָּו׃ 7 וַיֹּאמֶר יִצְחָק אֶל־אַבְרָהָם אָבִיו וַיֹּאמֶר אָבִי
וַיֹּאמֶר הִנֶּנִּי בְנִי וַיֹּאמֶר הִנֵּה הָאֵשׁ וְהָעֵצִים וְאַיֵּה הַשֶּׂה לְעֹלָה׃
8 וַיֹּאמֶר אַבְרָהָם אֱלֹהִים יִרְאֶה־לּוֹ הַשֶּׂה לְעֹלָה בְּנִי וַיֵּלְכוּ שְׁנֵיהֶם
יַחְדָּו׃ 9 [11]וַיָּבֹאוּ אֶל־הַמָּקוֹם אֲשֶׁר אָמַר־לוֹ הָאֱלֹהִים [12]וַיִּבֶן שָׁם
אַבְרָהָם אֶת־הַמִּזְבֵּחַ וַיַּעֲרֹךְ אֶת־הָעֵצִים וַיַּעֲקֹד אֶת־יִצְחָק בְּנוֹ וַיָּשֶׂם
אֹתוֹ עַל־הַמִּזְבֵּחַ מִמַּעַל לָעֵצִים׃ 10 וַיִּשְׁלַח אַבְרָהָם אֶת־יָדוֹ
וַיִּקַּח אֶת־הַמַּאֲכֶלֶת לִשְׁחֹט אֶת־בְּנוֹ׃ 11 וַיִּקְרָא אֵלָיו מַלְאַךְ יְהוָה
מִן־הַשָּׁמַיִם וַיֹּאמֶר אַבְרָהָם אַבְרָהָם וַיֹּאמֶר הִנֵּנִי׃ 12 וַיֹּאמֶר אַל־
תִּשְׁלַח יָדְךָ אֶל־הַנַּעַר וְאַל־[13]תַּעַשׂ לוֹ מְאוּמָה כִּי עַתָּה יָדַעְתִּי כִּי־
יְרֵא אֱלֹהִים אַתָּה וְלֹא חָשַׂכְתָּ אֶת־בִּנְךָ אֶת־יְחִידְךָ מִמֶּנִּי׃ 13 וַיִּשָּׂא

אַבְרָהָם אֶת־עֵינָיו וַיַּרְא וְהִנֵּה־אַיִל אַחַר נֶאֱחַז בַּסְּבַךְ בְּקַרְנָיו וַיֵּלֶךְ
אַבְרָהָם וַיִּקַּח אֶת־הָאַיִל וַיַּעֲלֵהוּ לְעֹלָה תַּחַת בְּנוֹ׃ 14 וַיִּקְרָא
אַבְרָהָם שֵׁם־הַמָּקוֹם הַהוּא יְהוָה יִרְאֶה אֲשֶׁר יֵאָמֵר הַיּוֹם בְּהַר
יְהוָה יֵרָאֶה׃

1. לָקַח. 2. יָלַךְ 3 עָלָה 4 קוּם 5. נָשָׂא. 6 רָאָה 7 יָשַׁב
8 יָלַךְ. 9 שָׁתָה 10 שִׂים 11 בּוֹא 12 בָּנָה 13 עָשָׂה

ג   מֹשֶׁה׃

1 וּמֹשֶׁה הָיָה רֹעֶה אֶת־צֹאן יִתְרוֹ חֹתְנוֹ כֹּהֵן מִדְיָן וַיִּנְהַג
אֶת־הַצֹּאן אַחַר הַמִּדְבָּר וַיָּבֹא אֶל־הַר הָאֱלֹהִים חֹרֵבָה׃ 2 וַיֵּרָא
מַלְאַךְ יְהוָה אֵלָיו בְּלַבַּת־אֵשׁ מִתּוֹךְ הַסְּנֶה וַיַּרְא וְהִנֵּה הַסְּנֶה בֹּעֵר
בָּאֵשׁ וְהַסְּנֶה אֵינֶנּוּ אֻכָּל׃ 3 וַיֹּאמֶר מֹשֶׁה אָסֻרָה־נָּא וְאֶרְאֶה אֶת־
הַמַּרְאֶה הַגָּדֹל הַזֶּה מַדּוּעַ לֹא־יִבְעַר הַסְּנֶה׃ 4 וַיַּרְא יְהוָה כִּי סָר
לִרְאוֹת וַיִּקְרָא אֵלָיו אֱלֹהִים מִתּוֹךְ הַסְּנֶה וַיֹּאמֶר מֹשֶׁה מֹשֶׁה וַיֹּאמֶר
הִנֵּנִי׃ 5 וַיֹּאמֶר אַל־תִּקְרַב הֲלֹם שַׁל־נְעָלֶיךָ מֵעַל רַגְלֶיךָ כִּי הַמָּקוֹם
אֲשֶׁר אַתָּה עוֹמֵד עָלָיו אַדְמַת־קֹדֶשׁ הוּא׃ 6 וַיֹּאמֶר אָנֹכִי אֱלֹהֵי
אָבִיךָ אֱלֹהֵי אַבְרָהָם אֱלֹהֵי יִצְחָק וֵאלֹהֵי יַעֲקֹב וַיַּסְתֵּר מֹשֶׁה פָּנָיו
כִּי יָרֵא מֵהַבִּיט אֶל־הָאֱלֹהִים׃ 7 וַיֹּאמֶר יְהוָה רָאֹה רָאִיתִי אֶת־
עֳנִי עַמִּי אֲשֶׁר בְּמִצְרָיִם וְאֶת־צַעֲקָתָם שָׁמַעְתִּי מִפְּנֵי נֹגְשָׂיו כִּי יָדַעְתִּי
אֶת־מַכְאֹבָיו׃ 8 וָאֵרֵד לְהַצִּילוֹ מִיַּד מִצְרַיִם וּלְהַעֲלֹתוֹ מִן־הָאָרֶץ
הַהִוא אֶל־אֶרֶץ טוֹבָה וּרְחָבָה אֶל־אֶרֶץ זָבַת חָלָב וּדְבַשׁ אֶל־מְקוֹם
הַכְּנַעֲנִי וְהַחִתִּי וְהָאֱמֹרִי וְהַפְּרִזִּי וְהַחִוִּי וְהַיְבוּסִי׃ 9 וְעַתָּה הִנֵּה
צַעֲקַת בְּנֵי־יִשְׂרָאֵל בָּאָה אֵלָי וְגַם־רָאִיתִי אֶת־הַלַּחַץ אֲשֶׁר מִצְרַיִם
לֹחֲצִים אֹתָם׃ 10 וְעַתָּה לְכָה וְאֶשְׁלָחֲךָ אֶל־פַּרְעֹה וְהוֹצֵא אֶת־
עַמִּי בְנֵי־יִשְׂרָאֵל מִמִּצְרָיִם׃ 11 וַיֹּאמֶר מֹשֶׁה אֶל־הָאֱלֹהִים מִי
אָנֹכִי כִּי אֵלֵךְ אֶל־פַּרְעֹה וְכִי אוֹצִיא אֶת־בְּנֵי יִשְׂרָאֵל מִמִּצְרָיִם׃
12 וַיֹּאמֶר כִּי־אֶהְיֶה עִמָּךְ וְזֶה־לְּךָ הָאוֹת כִּי אָנֹכִי שְׁלַחְתִּיךָ
בְּהוֹצִיאֲךָ אֶת־הָעָם מִמִּצְרַיִם תַּעַבְדוּן אֶת־הָאֱלֹהִים עַל הָהָר הַזֶּה׃
13 וַיֹּאמֶר מֹשֶׁה אֶל־הָאֱלֹהִים הִנֵּה אָנֹכִי בָא אֶל־בְּנֵי יִשְׂרָאֵל וְאָמַרְתִּי
לָהֶם אֱלֹהֵי אֲבוֹתֵיכֶם שְׁלָחַנִי אֲלֵיכֶם וְאָמְרוּ־לִי מַה־שְּׁמוֹ מָה אֹמַר
אֲלֵהֶם׃ 14 וַיֹּאמֶר אֱלֹהִים אֶל־מֹשֶׁה אֶהְיֶה אֲשֶׁר אֶהְיֶה וַיֹּאמֶר

כֹּה תֹאמַר לִבְנֵי יִשְׂרָאֵל אֶהְיֶה שְׁלָחַנִי אֲלֵיכֶם: 15 וַיֹּאמֶר עוֹד
אֱלֹהִים אֶל־מֹשֶׁה כֹּה תֹאמַר אֶל־בְּנֵי יִשְׂרָאֵל יהוָה אֱלֹהֵי אֲבֹתֵיכֶם
אֱלֹהֵי אַבְרָהָם אֱלֹהֵי יִצְחָק וֵאלֹהֵי יַעֲקֹב שְׁלָחַנִי אֲלֵיכֶם זֶה־שְּׁמִי
לְעֹלָם וְזֶה זִכְרִי לְדֹר דֹּר:

ד   שְׁמוּאֵל:

1 וְהַנַּעַר שְׁמוּאֵל מְשָׁרֵת אֶת־יהוָה לִפְנֵי עֵלִי וּדְבַר יהוָה הָיָה
יָקָר בַּיָּמִים הָהֵם אֵין חָזוֹן נִפְרָץ: 2 וַיְהִי בַּיּוֹם הַהוּא וְעֵלִי שֹׁכֵב
בִּמְקֹמוֹ וְעֵינָיו הֵחֵלּוּ כֵהוֹת לֹא יוּכַל לִרְאוֹת: 3 וְנֵר אֱלֹהִים טֶרֶם
יִכְבֶּה וּשְׁמוּאֵל שֹׁכֵב בְּהֵיכַל יהוָה אֲשֶׁר־שָׁם אֲרוֹן אֱלֹהִים: 4 וַיִּקְרָא
יהוָה אֶל־שְׁמוּאֵל וַיֹּאמֶר הִנֵּנִי: 5 וַיָּרָץ אֶל־עֵלִי וַיֹּאמֶר הִנְנִי כִּי־
קָרָאתָ לִּי וַיֹּאמֶר לֹא־קָרָאתִי שׁוּב שְׁכָב וַיֵּלֶךְ וַיִּשְׁכָּב: 6 וַיֹּסֶף יהוָה
קְרֹא עוֹד שְׁמוּאֵל וַיָּקָם שְׁמוּאֵל וַיֵּלֶךְ אֶל־עֵלִי וַיֹּאמֶר הִנְנִי כִּי קָרָאתָ
לִי וַיֹּאמֶר לֹא־קָרָאתִי בְנִי שׁוּב שְׁכָב: 7 וּשְׁמוּאֵל טֶרֶם יָדַע אֶת־
יהוָה וְטֶרֶם יִגָּלֶה אֵלָיו דְּבַר־יהוָה: 8 וַיֹּסֶף יהוָה קְרֹא־שְׁמוּאֵל
בַּשְּׁלִשִׁת וַיָּקָם וַיֵּלֶךְ אֶל־עֵלִי וַיֹּאמֶר הִנְנִי כִּי קָרָאתָ לִי וַיָּבֶן עֵלִי
כִּי יהוָה קֹרֵא לַנָּעַר: 9 וַיֹּאמֶר עֵלִי לִשְׁמוּאֵל לֵךְ שְׁכָב וְהָיָה אִם־
יִקְרָא אֵלֶיךָ וְאָמַרְתָּ דַּבֵּר יהוָה כִּי שֹׁמֵעַ עַבְדֶּךָ וַיֵּלֶךְ שְׁמוּאֵל וַיִּשְׁכַּב
בִּמְקֹמוֹ: 10 וַיָּבֹא יהוָה וַיִּתְיַצַּב וַיִּקְרָא כְפַעַם־בְּפַעַם שְׁמוּאֵל
שְׁמוּאֵל וַיֹּאמֶר שְׁמוּאֵל דַּבֵּר כִּי שֹׁמֵעַ עַבְדֶּךָ: 11 וַיֹּאמֶר יהוָה אֶל־
שְׁמוּאֵל הִנֵּה אָנֹכִי עֹשֶׂה דָבָר בְּיִשְׂרָאֵל אֲשֶׁר כָּל־שֹׁמְעוֹ תְּצִלֶּינָה
שְׁתֵּי אָזְנָיו: 12 בַּיּוֹם הַהוּא אָקִים אֶל־עֵלִי אֵת כָּל־אֲשֶׁר דִּבַּרְתִּי
אֶל־בֵּיתוֹ הָחֵל וְכַלֵּה: 13 וְהִגַּדְתִּי לוֹ כִּי־שֹׁפֵט אֲנִי אֶת־בֵּיתוֹ עַד־
עוֹלָם בַּעֲוֺן אֲשֶׁר־יָדַע כִּי־מְקַלְלִים לָהֶם בָּנָיו וְלֹא כִהָה בָּם: 14 וְלָכֵן
נִשְׁבַּעְתִּי לְבֵית עֵלִי אִם־יִתְכַּפֵּר עֲוֺן בֵּית־עֵלִי בְּזֶבַח וּבְמִנְחָה עַד־
עוֹלָם: 15 וַיִּשְׁכַּב שְׁמוּאֵל עַד־הַבֹּקֶר וַיִּפְתַּח אֶת־דַּלְתוֹת בֵּית־יהוָה
וּשְׁמוּאֵל יָרֵא מֵהַגִּיד אֶת־הַמַּרְאָה אֶל־עֵלִי: 16 וַיִּקְרָא עֵלִי אֶת־
שְׁמוּאֵל וַיֹּאמֶר שְׁמוּאֵל בְּנִי וַיֹּאמֶר הִנֵּנִי: 17 וַיֹּאמֶר מָה הַדָּבָר
אֲשֶׁר דִּבֶּר אֵלֶיךָ אַל־נָא תְכַחֵד מִמֶּנִּי כֹּה יַעֲשֶׂה־לְּךָ אֱלֹהִים וְכֹה
יוֹסִיף אִם־תְּכַחֵד מִמֶּנִּי דָּבָר מִכָּל־הַדָּבָר אֲשֶׁר־דִּבֶּר אֵלֶיךָ: 18 וַיַּגֶּד־
לוֹ שְׁמוּאֵל אֶת־כָּל־הַדְּבָרִים וְלֹא כִחֵד מִמֶּנּוּ וַיֹּאמֶר יהוָה הוּא הַטּוֹב

19 וַיִּגְדַּל֙ שְׁמוּאֵ֔ל וַֽיהֹוָה֙ הָיָ֣ה עִמּ֔וֹ וְלֹֽא־הִפִּ֖יל בְּעֵינָ֖יו יַעֲשֶֽׂה׃ 20 וַיֵּ֙דַע֙ כָּל־יִשְׂרָאֵ֔ל מִדָּ֖ן וְעַד־בְּאֵ֣ר שָׁ֑בַע כִּ֚י נֶאֱמָ֣ן שְׁמוּאֵ֔ל לְנָבִ֖יא לַֽיהֹוָֽה׃ 21 וַיֹּ֥סֶף יְהֹוָ֖ה לְהֵרָאֹ֣ה בְשִׁלֹ֑ה כִּֽי־נִגְלָ֤ה יְהֹוָה֙ אֶל־שְׁמוּאֵ֔ל בְּשִׁל֖וֹ בִּדְבַ֥ר יְהֹוָֽה׃

ה   עֵלִֽי׃

1 וַיְהִ֥י דְבַר־שְׁמוּאֵ֖ל לְכָל־יִשְׂרָאֵ֑ל וַיֵּצֵ֣א יִשְׂרָאֵל֩ לִקְרַ֨את פְּלִשְׁתִּ֜ים לַמִּלְחָמָ֗ה וַֽיַּחֲנוּ֙ עַל־הָאֶ֣בֶן הָעֵ֔זֶר וּפְלִשְׁתִּ֖ים חָנ֥וּ בַאֲפֵֽק׃ 2 וַיַּעַרְכ֨וּ פְלִשְׁתִּ֜ים לִקְרַ֣את יִשְׂרָאֵ֗ל וַתִּטֹּשׁ֙ הַמִּלְחָמָ֔ה וַיִּנָּ֥גֶף יִשְׂרָאֵ֖ל לִפְנֵ֣י פְלִשְׁתִּ֑ים וַיַּכּ֤וּ בַמַּֽעֲרָכָה֙ בַּשָּׂדֶ֔ה כְּאַרְבַּ֥עַת אֲלָפִ֖ים אִֽישׁ׃ 3 וַיָּבֹ֣א הָעָ֗ם אֶל־הַֽמַּחֲנֶה֒ וַיֹּֽאמְרוּ֙ זִקְנֵ֣י יִשְׂרָאֵ֔ל לָ֣מָּה נְגָפָ֧נוּ יְהֹוָ֛ה הַיּ֖וֹם לִפְנֵ֣י פְלִשְׁתִּ֑ים נִקְחָ֧ה אֵלֵ֣ינוּ מִשִּׁלֹ֗ה אֶת־אֲרוֹן֙ בְּרִ֣ית יְהֹוָ֔ה וְיָבֹ֣א בְקִרְבֵּ֔נוּ וְיֹשִׁעֵ֖נוּ מִכַּ֥ף אֹיְבֵֽינוּ׃ × 4 וַיִּשְׁלַ֤ח הָעָם֙ שִׁלֹ֔ה וַיִּשְׂא֣וּ מִשָּׁ֗ם אֵ֚ת אֲר֣וֹן בְּרִית־יְהֹוָ֣ה צְבָא֔וֹת יֹשֵׁ֖ב הַכְּרֻבִ֑ים וְשָׁ֞ם שְׁנֵ֣י בְנֵֽי־עֵלִ֗י עִם־אֲרוֹן֙ בְּרִ֣ית הָֽאֱלֹהִ֔ים חָפְנִ֖י וּפִֽינְחָֽס׃ 5 וַיְהִ֗י כְּב֨וֹא אֲר֤וֹן בְּרִית־יְהֹוָה֙ אֶל־הַֽמַּחֲנֶ֔ה וַיָּרִ֥עוּ כָל־יִשְׂרָאֵ֖ל תְּרוּעָ֣ה גְדוֹלָ֑ה וַתֵּהֹ֖ם הָאָֽרֶץ׃ 6 וַיִּשְׁמְע֤וּ פְלִשְׁתִּים֙ אֶת־ק֣וֹל הַתְּרוּעָ֔ה וַיֹּ֣אמְר֔וּ מֶ֠ה ק֣וֹל הַתְּרוּעָ֧ה הַגְּדוֹלָ֛ה הַזֹּ֖את בְּמַחֲנֵ֣ה הָעִבְרִ֑ים וַיֵּ֣דְע֔וּ כִּ֚י אֲר֣וֹן יְהֹוָ֔ה בָּ֖א אֶל־הַֽמַּחֲנֶֽה׃ 7 וַיִּֽרְא֣וּ הַפְּלִשְׁתִּ֔ים כִּ֣י אָֽמְר֔וּ בָּ֥א אֱלֹהִ֖ים אֶל־הַֽמַּחֲנֶ֑ה וַיֹּֽאמְרוּ֙ א֣וֹי לָ֔נוּ כִּ֣י לֹ֥א הָֽיְתָ֛ה כָּזֹ֖את אֶתְמ֥וֹל שִׁלְשֹֽׁם׃ 8 א֣וֹי לָ֔נוּ מִ֣י יַצִּילֵ֔נוּ מִיַּ֛ד הָאֱלֹהִ֥ים הָאַדִּירִ֖ים הָאֵ֑לֶּה אֵ֣לֶּה הֵ֗ם הָאֱלֹהִ֞ים הַמַּכִּ֧ים אֶת־מִצְרַ֛יִם בְּכָל־מַכָּ֖ה בַּמִּדְבָּֽר׃ 9 הִֽתְחַזְּק֞וּ וִֽהְי֤וּ לַֽאֲנָשִׁים֙ פְּלִשְׁתִּ֔ים פֶּ֚ן תַּעַבְד֣וּ לָעִבְרִ֔ים כַּאֲשֶׁ֥ר עָבְד֖וּ לָכֶ֑ם וִהְיִיתֶ֥ם לַֽאֲנָשִׁ֖ים וְנִלְחַמְתֶּֽם׃ 10 וַיִּלָּֽחֲמ֣וּ פְלִשְׁתִּ֗ים וַיִּנָּ֤גֶף יִשְׂרָאֵל֙ וַיָּנֻ֙סוּ֙ אִ֣ישׁ לְאֹֽהָלָ֔יו וַתְּהִ֥י הַמַּכָּ֖ה גְדוֹלָ֣ה מְאֹ֑ד וַיִּפֹּל֙ מִיִּשְׂרָאֵ֔ל שְׁלֹשִׁ֖ים אֶ֥לֶף רַגְלִֽי׃ 11 וַאֲר֥וֹן אֱלֹהִ֖ים נִלְקָ֑ח וּשְׁנֵ֧י בְנֵֽי־עֵלִ֛י מֵ֖תוּ חָפְנִ֥י וּפִֽינְחָֽס׃ 12 וַיָּ֤רׇץ אִישׁ־בִּנְיָמִן֙ מֵהַמַּ֣עֲרָכָ֔ה וַיָּבֹ֥א שִׁלֹ֖ה בַּיּ֣וֹם הַה֑וּא וּמַדָּ֣יו קְרֻעִ֔ים וַאֲדָמָ֖ה עַל־רֹאשֽׁוֹ׃ 13 וַיָּב֗וֹא וְהִנֵּ֣ה עֵלִ֗י יֹשֵׁ֤ב עַל־הַכִּסֵּא֙ יַ֣ד דֶּ֣רֶךְ מְצַפֶּ֔ה כִּֽי־הָיָ֤ה לִבּוֹ֙ חָרֵ֔ד עַ֖ל אֲר֣וֹן הָאֱלֹהִ֑ים וְהָאִ֗ישׁ בָּ֚א לְהַגִּ֣יד בָּעִ֔יר וַתִּזְעַ֖ק כָּל־הָעִֽיר׃ 14 וַיִּשְׁמַ֤ע עֵלִי֙ אֶת־ק֣וֹל הַצְּעָקָ֔ה וַיֹּ֕אמֶר מֶ֛ה ק֥וֹל הֶהָמ֖וֹן הַזֶּ֑ה וְהָאִ֣ישׁ מִהַ֔ר וַיָּבֹ֖א וַיַּגֵּ֥ד לְעֵלִֽי׃ 15 וְעֵלִ֕י בֶּן־תִּשְׁעִ֥ים וּשְׁמֹנֶ֖ה שָׁנָ֑ה

וְעֵינָיו קָמָה וְלֹא יָכוֹל לִרְאוֹת׃ 16 וַיֹּאמֶר הָאִישׁ אֶל־עֵלִי אָנֹכִי
הַבָּא מִן־הַמַּעֲרָכָה וַאֲנִי מִן־הַמַּעֲרָכָה נַסְתִּי הַיּוֹם וַיֹּאמֶר מֶה־הָיָה
הַדָּבָר בְּנִי׃ 17 וַיַּעַן הַמְבַשֵּׂר וַיֹּאמֶר נָס יִשְׂרָאֵל לִפְנֵי פְלִשְׁתִּים
וְגַם מַגֵּפָה גְדוֹלָה הָיְתָה בָעָם וְגַם־שְׁנֵי בָנֶיךָ מֵתוּ חָפְנִי וּפִינְחָס
וַאֲרוֹן הָאֱלֹהִים נִלְקָחָה׃ 18 וַיְהִי כְּהַזְכִּירוֹ אֶת־אֲרוֹן הָאֱלֹהִים
וַיִּפֹּל מֵעַל־הַכִּסֵּא אֲחֹרַנִּית בְּעַד יַד הַשַּׁעַר וַתִּשָּׁבֵר מַפְרַקְתּוֹ וַיָּמֹת
כִּי־זָקֵן הָאִישׁ וְכָבֵד וְהוּא שָׁפַט אֶת־יִשְׂרָאֵל אַרְבָּעִים שָׁנָה׃

ר   יוֹסֵף׃

1 וְלֹא־יָכֹל יוֹסֵף לְהִתְאַפֵּק לְכֹל הַנִּצָּבִים עָלָיו וַיִּקְרָא הוֹצִיאוּ
כָל־אִישׁ מֵעָלָי וְלֹא־עָמַד אִישׁ אִתּוֹ בְּהִתְוַדַּע יוֹסֵף אֶל־אֶחָיו׃ 2 וַיִּתֵּן
אֶת־קֹלוֹ בִּבְכִי וַיִּשְׁמְעוּ מִצְרַיִם וַיִּשְׁמַע בֵּית פַּרְעֹה׃ 3 וַיֹּאמֶר יוֹסֵף
אֶל־אֶחָיו אֲנִי יוֹסֵף הַעוֹד אָבִי חָי וְלֹא־יָכְלוּ אֶחָיו לַעֲנוֹת אֹתוֹ כִּי
נִבְהֲלוּ מִפָּנָיו׃ 4 וַיֹּאמֶר יוֹסֵף אֶל־אֶחָיו גְּשׁוּ־נָא אֵלַי וַיִּגָּשׁוּ וַיֹּאמֶר
אֲנִי יוֹסֵף אֲחִיכֶם אֲשֶׁר־מְכַרְתֶּם אֹתִי מִצְרָיְמָה׃ 5 וְעַתָּה אַל־תֵּעָצְבוּ
וְאַל־יִחַר בְּעֵינֵיכֶם כִּי־מְכַרְתֶּם אֹתִי הֵנָּה כִּי לְמִחְיָה שְׁלָחַנִי אֱלֹהִים
לִפְנֵיכֶם׃ 6 כִּי־זֶה שְׁנָתַיִם הָרָעָב בְּקֶרֶב הָאָרֶץ וְעוֹד חָמֵשׁ שָׁנִים
אֲשֶׁר אֵין־חָרִישׁ וְקָצִיר׃ 7 וַיִּשְׁלָחֵנִי אֱלֹהִים לִפְנֵיכֶם לָשׂוּם לָכֶם
שְׁאֵרִית בָּאָרֶץ וּלְהַחֲיוֹת לָכֶם לִפְלֵיטָה גְּדֹלָה׃ 8 וְעַתָּה לֹא־אַתֶּם
שְׁלַחְתֶּם אֹתִי הֵנָּה כִּי הָאֱלֹהִים וַיְשִׂימֵנִי לְאָב לְפַרְעֹה וּלְאָדוֹן
לְכָל־בֵּיתוֹ וּמֹשֵׁל בְּכָל־אֶרֶץ מִצְרָיִם׃ 9 מַהֲרוּ וַעֲלוּ אֶל־אָבִי
וַאֲמַרְתֶּם אֵלָיו כֹּה אָמַר בִּנְךָ יוֹסֵף שָׂמַנִי אֱלֹהִים לְאָדוֹן לְכָל־מִצְרָיִם
רְדָה אֵלַי אַל־תַּעֲמֹד׃ 10 וְיָשַׁבְתָּ בְאֶרֶץ־גֹּשֶׁן וְהָיִיתָ קָרוֹב אֵלַי
אַתָּה וּבָנֶיךָ וּבְנֵי בָנֶיךָ וְצֹאנְךָ וּבְקָרְךָ וְכָל־אֲשֶׁר־לָךְ׃ 11 וְכִלְכַּלְתִּי
אֹתְךָ שָׁם כִּי־עוֹד חָמֵשׁ שָׁנִים רָעָב פֶּן־תִּוָּרֵשׁ אַתָּה וּבֵיתְךָ וְכָל־אֲשֶׁר־
לָךְ׃ 12 וְהִנֵּה עֵינֵיכֶם רֹאוֹת וְעֵינֵי אָחִי בִנְיָמִין כִּי־פִי הַמְדַבֵּר
אֲלֵיכֶם׃ 13 וְהִגַּדְתֶּם לְאָבִי אֶת־כָּל־כְּבוֹדִי בְּמִצְרַיִם וְאֵת כָּל־אֲשֶׁר
רְאִיתֶם וּמִהַרְתֶּם וְהוֹרַדְתֶּם אֶת־אָבִי הֵנָּה׃ 14 וַיִּפֹּל עַל־צַוְּארֵי
בִנְיָמִן־אָחִיו וַיֵּבְךְּ וּבִנְיָמִן בָּכָה עַל־צַוָּארָיו׃ 15 וַיְנַשֵּׁק לְכָל־אֶחָיו
וַיֵּבְךְּ עֲלֵהֶם וְאַחֲרֵי כֵן דִּבְּרוּ אֶחָיו אִתּוֹ׃

ז   יִשְׂרָאֵל:

1 וְהַקֹּל נִשְׁמַע בֵּית פַּרְעֹה לֵאמֹר בָּאוּ אֲחֵי יוֹסֵף וַיִּיטַב בְּעֵינֵי
פַרְעֹה וּבְעֵינֵי עֲבָדָיו: 2 וַיֹּאמֶר פַּרְעֹה אֶל־יוֹסֵף אֱמֹר אֶל־אַחֶיךָ
זֹאת עֲשׂוּ טַעֲנוּ אֶת־בְּעִירְכֶם וּלְכוּ־בֹאוּ אַרְצָה כְּנָעַן: 3 וּקְחוּ אֶת־
אֲבִיכֶם וְאֶת־בָּתֵּיכֶם וּבֹאוּ אֵלָי וְאֶתְּנָה לָכֶם אֶת־טוּב אֶרֶץ מִצְרַיִם
וְאִכְלוּ אֶת־חֵלֶב הָאָרֶץ: 4 וְאַתָּה צֻוֵּיתָה זֹאת עֲשׂוּ קְחוּ־לָכֶם
מֵאֶרֶץ מִצְרַיִם עֲגָלוֹת לְטַפְּכֶם וְלִנְשֵׁיכֶם וּנְשָׂאתֶם אֶת־אֲבִיכֶם וּבָאתֶם:
5 וְעֵינְכֶם אַל־תָּחֹס עַל־כְּלֵיכֶם כִּי־טוּב כָּל־אֶרֶץ מִצְרַיִם לָכֶם הוּא:
6 וַיַּעֲשׂוּ־כֵן בְּנֵי יִשְׂרָאֵל וַיִּתֵּן לָהֶם יוֹסֵף עֲגָלוֹת עַל־פִּי פַרְעֹה
וַיִּתֵּן לָהֶם צֵדָה לַדָּרֶךְ: 7 לְכֻלָּם נָתַן לָאִישׁ חֲלִפוֹת שְׂמָלֹת
וּלְבִנְיָמִן נָתַן שְׁלֹשׁ מֵאוֹת כֶּסֶף וְחָמֵשׁ חֲלִפֹת שְׂמָלֹת: 8 וּלְאָבִיו
שָׁלַח כְּזֹאת עֲשָׂרָה חֲמֹרִים נֹשְׂאִים מִטּוּב מִצְרָיִם וְעֶשֶׂר אֲתֹנֹת
נֹשְׂאֹת בָּר וָלֶחֶם וּמָזוֹן לְאָבִיו לַדָּרֶךְ: 9 וַיְשַׁלַּח אֶת־אֶחָיו וַיֵּלֵכוּ
וַיֹּאמֶר אֲלֵהֶם אַל־תִּרְגְּזוּ בַּדָּרֶךְ: 10 וַיַּעֲלוּ מִמִּצְרָיִם וַיָּבֹאוּ אֶרֶץ
כְּנַעַן אֶל־יַעֲקֹב אֲבִיהֶם: 11 וַיַּגִּדוּ לוֹ לֵאמֹר עוֹד יוֹסֵף חַי וְכִי־
הוּא מֹשֵׁל בְּכָל־אֶרֶץ מִצְרָיִם וַיָּפָג לִבּוֹ כִּי לֹא־הֶאֱמִין לָהֶם:
12 וַיְדַבְּרוּ אֵלָיו אֵת כָּל־דִּבְרֵי יוֹסֵף אֲשֶׁר דִּבֶּר אֲלֵהֶם וַיַּרְא אֶת־
הָעֲגָלוֹת אֲשֶׁר־שָׁלַח יוֹסֵף לָשֵׂאת אֹתוֹ וַתְּחִי רוּחַ יַעֲקֹב אֲבִיהֶם:
13 וַיֹּאמֶר יִשְׂרָאֵל רַב עוֹד־יוֹסֵף בְּנִי חָי אֵלְכָה וְאֶרְאֶנּוּ בְּטֶרֶם
אָמוּת: 14 וַיִּסַּע יִשְׂרָאֵל וְכָל־אֲשֶׁר־לוֹ וַיָּבֹא בְּאֵרָה שָּׁבַע וַיִּזְבַּח
זְבָחִים לֵאלֹהֵי אָבִיו יִצְחָק: 15 וַיֹּאמֶר אֱלֹהִים לְיִשְׂרָאֵל בְּמַרְאֹת
הַלַּיְלָה וַיֹּאמֶר יַעֲקֹב יַעֲקֹב וַיֹּאמֶר הִנֵּנִי: 16 וַיֹּאמֶר אָנֹכִי הָאֵל אֱלֹהֵי
אָבִיךָ אַל־תִּירָא מֵרְדָה מִצְרַיְמָה כִּי־לְגוֹי גָּדוֹל אֲשִׂימְךָ שָׁם:
17 אָנֹכִי אֵרֵד עִמְּךָ מִצְרַיְמָה וְאָנֹכִי אַעַלְךָ גַם־עָלֹה וְיוֹסֵף יָשִׁית
יָדוֹ עַל־עֵינֶיךָ: 18 וַיָּקָם יַעֲקֹב מִבְּאֵר שָׁבַע וַיִּשְׂאוּ בְנֵי־יִשְׂרָאֵל
אֶת־יַעֲקֹב אֲבִיהֶם וְאֶת־טַפָּם וְאֶת־נְשֵׁיהֶם בָּעֲגָלוֹת אֲשֶׁר־שָׁלַח פַּרְעֹה
לָשֵׂאת אֹתוֹ: 19 וַיִּקְחוּ אֶת־מִקְנֵיהֶם וְאֶת־רְכוּשָׁם אֲשֶׁר רָכְשׁוּ
בְּאֶרֶץ כְּנַעַן וַיָּבֹאוּ מִצְרָיְמָה יַעֲקֹב וְכָל־זַרְעוֹ אִתּוֹ: 20 בָּנָיו וּבְנֵי
בָנָיו אִתּוֹ בְּנֹתָיו וּבְנוֹת בָּנָיו וְכָל־זַרְעוֹ הֵבִיא אִתּוֹ מִצְרָיְמָה:

ח   (*דָוִד וְגָלְיָת:

1 וַיֹּאמֶר שָׁאוּל אֶל־דָּוִד לֹא תוּכַל לָלֶכֶת אֶל־הַפְּלִשְׁתִּי הַזֶּה
לְהִלָּחֵם עִמּוֹ כִּי־נַעַר אַתָּה וְהוּא אִישׁ מִלְחָמָה מִנְּעֻרָיו: 2 וַיֹּאמֶר
דָּוִד אֶל־שָׁאוּל רֹעֶה הָיָה עַבְדְּךָ לְאָבִיו בַּצֹּאן וּבָא הָאֲרִי וְאֶת־הַדּוֹב
וְנָשָׂא שֶׂה מֵהָעֵדֶר: 3 וְיָצָאתִי אַחֲרָיו וְהִכִּתִיו וְהִצַּלְתִּי מִפִּיו
וַיָּקָם עָלַי וְהֶחֱזַקְתִּי בִּזְקָנוֹ וְהִכִּתִיו וַהֲמִיתִּיו: X 4 גַּם אֶת־הָאֲרִי
גַּם־הַדּוֹב הִכָּה עַבְדֶּךָ וְהָיָה הַפְּלִשְׁתִּי הֶעָרֵל הַזֶּה כְּאַחַד מֵהֶם כִּי
חֵרֵף מַעַרְכֹת אֱלֹהִים חַיִּים: 5 וַיֹּאמֶר דָּוִד יְהוָה אֲשֶׁר הִצִּלַנִי
מִיַּד הָאֲרִי וּמִיַּד הַדֹּב הוּא יַצִּילֵנִי מִיַּד הַפְּלִשְׁתִּי הַזֶּה ○ וַיֹּאמֶר
שָׁאוּל אֶל־דָּוִד לֵךְ וַיהוָה יִהְיֶה עִמָּךְ: 6 וַיַּלְבֵּשׁ שָׁאוּל אֶת־דָּוִד
מַדָּיו וְנָתַן קוֹבַע נְחֹשֶׁת עַל־רֹאשׁוֹ וַיַּלְבֵּשׁ אֹתוֹ שִׁרְיוֹן: 7 וַיַּחְגֹּר
דָּוִד אֶת־חַרְבּוֹ מֵעַל לְמַדָּיו וַיֹּאֶל לָלֶכֶת כִּי לֹא־נִסָּה וַיֹּאמֶר דָּוִד
אֶל־שָׁאוּל לֹא־אוּכַל לָלֶכֶת בָּאֵלֶּה כִּי לֹא נִסִּיתִי וַיְסִרֵם דָּוִד מֵעָלָיו:
8 וַיִּקַּח מַקְלוֹ בְּיָדוֹ וַיִּבְחַר־לוֹ חֲמִשָּׁה חַלֻּקֵי אֲבָנִים׀ מִן־הַנַּחַל
וַיָּשֶׂם אֹתָם בִּכְלִי הָרֹעִים אֲשֶׁר־לוֹ וּבַיַּלְקוּט וְקַלְעוֹ בְיָדוֹ וַיִּגַּשׁ אֶל־
הַפְּלִשְׁתִּי: 9 וַיֵּלֶךְ הַפְּלִשְׁתִּי הֹלֵךְ וְקָרֵב אֶל־דָּוִד וְהָאִישׁ נֹשֵׂא הַצִּנָּה
לְפָנָיו: 10 וַיַּבֵּט הַפְּלִשְׁתִּי וַיִּרְאֶה אֶת־דָּוִד וַיִּבְזֵהוּ כִּי־הָיָה נַעַר
וְאַדְמֹנִי עִם־יְפֵה מַרְאֶה: 11 וַיֹּאמֶר הַפְּלִשְׁתִּי אֶל־דָּוִד הַכֶלֶב
אָנֹכִי כִּי־אַתָּה בָא־אֵלַי בַּמַּקְלוֹת וַיְקַלֵּל הַפְּלִשְׁתִּי אֶת־דָּוִד בֵּאלֹהָיו:
12 וַיֹּאמֶר הַפְּלִשְׁתִּי אֶל־דָּוִד לְכָה אֵלַי וְאֶתְּנָה אֶת־בְּשָׂרְךָ לְעוֹף
הַשָּׁמַיִם וּלְבֶהֱמַת הַשָּׂדֶה: 13 וַיֹּאמֶר דָּוִד אֶל־הַפְּלִשְׁתִּי אַתָּה בָּא
אֵלַי בְּחֶרֶב וּבַחֲנִית וּבְכִידוֹן וְאָנֹכִי בָא־אֵלֶיךָ בְּשֵׁם יְהוָה צְבָאוֹת
אֱלֹהֵי מַעַרְכוֹת יִשְׂרָאֵל אֲשֶׁר חֵרַפְתָּ: 14 הַיּוֹם הַזֶּה יְסַגֶּרְךָ יְהוָה
בְּיָדִי וְהִכִּתִיךָ וַהֲסִרֹתִי אֶת־רֹאשְׁךָ מֵעָלֶיךָ וְנָתַתִּי פֶּגֶר מַחֲנֵה
פְלִשְׁתִּים הַיּוֹם הַזֶּה לְעוֹף הַשָּׁמַיִם וּלְחַיַּת הָאָרֶץ וְיֵדְעוּ כָּל־הָאָרֶץ
כִּי יֵשׁ אֱלֹהִים לְיִשְׂרָאֵל: ∧ 15 וְיֵדְעוּ כָּל־הַקָּהָל הַזֶּה כִּי־לֹא
בְּחֶרֶב וּבַחֲנִית יְהוֹשִׁיעַ יְהוָה כִּי לַיהוָה הַמִּלְחָמָה וְנָתַן אֶתְכֶם

*) These two last exercises are printed with all the accents
which had thus far been omitted

בְּיָדֵנוּ׃ 16 וְהָיָה כִּי־קָם הַפְּלִשְׁתִּי וַיֵּלֶךְ וַיִּקְרַב לִקְרַאת דָּוִד וַיְמַהֵר דָּוִד וַיָּרָץ הַמַּעֲרָכָה לִקְרַאת הַפְּלִשְׁתִּי׃ 17 וַיִּשְׁלַח דָּוִד אֶת־יָדוֹ אֶל־הַכְּלִי וַיִּקַּח מִשָּׁם אֶבֶן וַיְקַלַּע וַיַּךְ אֶת־הַפְּלִשְׁתִּי אֶל־מִצְחוֹ וַתִּטְבַּע הָאֶבֶן בְּמִצְחוֹ וַיִּפֹּל עַל־פָּנָיו אָרְצָה׃ 18 וַיֶּחֱזַק דָּוִד מִן־ הַפְּלִשְׁתִּי בַּקֶּלַע וּבָאֶבֶן וַיַּךְ אֶת־הַפְּלִשְׁתִּי וַיְמִתֵהוּ וְחֶרֶב אֵין בְּיַד־ דָּוִד׃ 19 וַיָּרָץ דָּוִד וַיַּעֲמֹד אֶל־הַפְּלִשְׁתִּי וַיִּקַּח אֶת־חַרְבּוֹ וַיִּשְׁלְפָהּ מִתַּעְרָהּ וַיְמֹתְתֵהוּ וַיִּכְרָת־בָּהּ אֶת־רֹאשׁוֹ וַיִּרְאוּ הַפְּלִשְׁתִּים כִּי־מֵת גִּבּוֹרָם וַיָּנֻסוּ׃

ט   דָּוִד וִיהוֹנָתָן׃

1 וַיִּקַּח דָּוִד אֶת־רֹאשׁ הַפְּלִשְׁתִּי וַיְבִאֵהוּ יְרוּשָׁלָ͏ִם וְאֶת־כֵּלָיו שָׂם בְּאָהֳלוֹ׃ 2 וְכִרְאוֹת שָׁאוּל אֶת־דָּוִד יֹצֵא לִקְרַאת הַפְּלִשְׁתִּי אָמַר אֶל־אַבְנֵר שַׂר הַצָּבָא בֶּן־מִי־זֶה הַנַּעַר אַבְנֵר וַיֹּאמֶר אַבְנֵר חֵי־ נַפְשְׁךָ הַמֶּלֶךְ אִם־יָדָעְתִּי׃ 3 וַיֹּאמֶר הַמֶּלֶךְ שְׁאַל אַתָּה בֶּן־מִי־זֶה הָעָלֶם׃ 4 וּכְשׁוּב דָּוִד מֵהַכּוֹת אֶת־הַפְּלִשְׁתִּי וַיִּקַּח אֹתוֹ אַבְנֵר וַיְבִאֵהוּ לִפְנֵי שָׁאוּל וְרֹאשׁ הַפְּלִשְׁתִּי בְּיָדוֹ׃ 5 וַיֹּאמֶר אֵלָיו שָׁאוּל בֶּן־מִי אַתָּה הַנַּעַר וַיֹּאמֶר דָּוִד בֶּן־עַבְדְּךָ יִשַׁי בֵּית הַלַּחְמִי׃ 6 וַיְהִי כְּכַלֹּתוֹ לְדַבֵּר אֶל־שָׁאוּל וְנֶפֶשׁ יְהוֹנָתָן נִקְשְׁרָה בְּנֶפֶשׁ דָּוִד וַיֶּאֱהָבֵהוּ יְהוֹנָתָן כְּנַפְשׁוֹ׃ 7 וַיִּקָּחֵהוּ שָׁאוּל בַּיּוֹם הַהוּא וְלֹא נְתָנוֹ לָשׁוּב בֵּית אָבִיו׃ 8 וַיִּכְרֹת יְהוֹנָתָן וְדָוִד בְּרִית בְּאַהֲבָתוֹ אֹתוֹ כְּנַפְשׁוֹ׃ 9 וַיִּתְפַּשֵּׁט יְהוֹנָתָן אֶת־הַמְּעִיל אֲשֶׁר עָלָיו וַיִּתְּנֵהוּ לְדָוִד וּמַדָּיו וְעַד־חַרְבּוֹ וְעַד־קַשְׁתּוֹ וְעַד־חֲגֹרוֹ׃ 10 וַיֵּצֵא דָוִד בְּכֹל אֲשֶׁר יִשְׁלָחֶנּוּ שָׁאוּל יַשְׂכִּיל וַיְשִׂמֵהוּ שָׁאוּל עַל אַנְשֵׁי הַמִּלְחָמָה וַיִּיטַב בְּעֵינֵי כָל־הָעָם וְגַם בְּעֵינֵי עַבְדֵי שָׁאוּל׃ 11 וַיְהִי בְּבוֹאָם בְּשׁוּב דָּוִד מֵהַכּוֹת אֶת־הַפְּלִשְׁתִּי וַתֵּצֶאנָה הַנָּשִׁים מִכָּל־עָרֵי יִשְׂרָאֵל לָשִׁיר וְהַמְּחֹלוֹת לִקְרַאת שָׁאוּל הַמֶּלֶךְ בְּתֻפִּים בְּשִׂמְחָה וּבְשָׁלִשִׁים׃ 12 וַתַּעֲנֶינָה הַנָּשִׁים הַמְשַׂחֲקוֹת וַתֹּאמַרְןָ הִכָּה שָׁאוּל בַּאֲלָפָו וְדָוִד בְּרִבְבֹתָיו׃ 13 וַיִּחַר לְשָׁאוּל מְאֹד וַיֵּרַע בְּעֵינָיו הַדָּבָר הַזֶּה וַיֹּאמֶר נָתְנוּ לְדָוִד רְבָבוֹת וְלִי נָתְנוּ הָאֲלָפִים וְעוֹד לוֹ אַךְ הַמְּלוּכָה׃ 14 וַיְהִי שָׁאוּל עֹיֵן אֶת־דָּוִד מֵהַיּוֹם הַהוּא וָהָלְאָה׃

v. 6.   v. 12. וַיְאֶהֱבֵהוּ קרי   בַּאֲלָפָיו ק׳.

VOCABULARY

OF THE WORDS OCCURRING IN THE EXERCISES.

אָב father (§ 69); *plur.* אָבוֹת fathers, ancestors

אָבַד he perished; *Pi* he destroyed, he killed

אֶבְיוֹן needy, poor

אֵבֶל mourning, misery

אֶבֶן עֵזֶר rock of help *(propr noun).*

אַבְרָם and אַבְרָהָם *propr noun* Abraham

אָדוֹן lord, master; *plur.* אֲדֹנָי God (§ 79, 2).

אַדִּיר great, powerful

אָדָם man, *coll* men

אֲדָמָה earth, dust

אַדְמֹנִי blonde, red.

אָהַב he loved

אֹהֶל tabernacle (אָהֳלִים *Syriasm*)

אוֹי *interj* woe!

אוֹצָר treasure; אָצַר accumulate

אוֹר *m.* and אוֹרָה *f* light (*pr inf* he shone, illumined).

אוֹת sign.

אָז *adv* then; מֵאָז *prep* and *conj.* from the time, when

אָזֵן *Hi* he listened, heard, lent his ears

אֹזֶן ear; *dual* אָזְנַיִם

אָח brother (§ 69)

אֶחָד one, somebody, any (§ 71).

אָחַז he caught, took hold

אַחַר 1 *adv a) of place:* from behind, behind; *commonly b) of time* afterwards, then 2 *prep.* after, behind; *plur* אַחֲרֵי is used as often, אַחֲרֵי כֵן, after (the thing) thus (happened) = afterwards

אַחֵר other, another.

אֲחֹרַנִּית backwards

אוֹיֵב enemy; אָיַב he opposed

אַךְ only, also, certainly

אַיֵּה where? (אֵי with He parag).

אַיִל ram.

אַיִן or אֵין (*pr subst.* defect, want, nothing) there is not, there was not (§ 96)

אִישׁ 1. man *coll.* men; 2. all, every one; *plur.* אֲנָשִׁים, *constr. stat.* אַנְשֵׁי (§ 69)

אִשָּׁה *f* from אִישׁ, woman (§ 69)

אָכַל he ate, dined, supped

אַל *conj* not (μή) especially before *fut.* (§ 96).

אֶל־ *prep*, to, into, against, towards, until among, besides, for, from

אֵל God (meaning the mighty one)

אֵלֶּה *pron plur comm*, these, those (§ 46)

אֱלוֹהַ God The plural אֱלֹהִים is used more frequently in the sense of the one God, as a singular (§ 79, 2)

אֶלֶף thousand

אִם 1 *conj* if, 2 in forms of swearing it has the power of a negation

אֵם mother, with *suff* אִמִּי

אָמֵן to be firm, certain, hence· he was faithful, true; *Ni* the same; *Hi* he believed

אָמַר 1 he said, spoke, 2 thought אֹמֶר and אִמְרָה speech, saying

אֱמֹרִי *n gent* Amorrhite, a Canaanite people

אֱמֶת faith, truth, fidelity, sincerity

אֱנוֹשׁ *plur.* אֲנָשִׁים man, same as אִישׁ

אֲנִי or אָנֹכִי I (pag 44)

אָפֵק he was strong, *Hithp* he fortified himself

אֲפֵק *propr. n.* city of Aphek

אַרְבַּע *m* אַרְבָּעָה *f* four; *plur.* אַרְבָּעִים forty

אֲרִי *fem* אַרְיֵה lion

אֲרוֹן chest, ark

אֹרַח path

אַרְכְלָאוֹס *propr n.* Archelaus

אֶרֶץ earth, land

אֵשׁ fire

אֲשֶׁר *pron rel* who, which (§ 47); כַּאֲשֶׁר like, as, when; בַּאֲשֶׁר where, because; עַד־אֲשֶׁר until; אֲשֶׁר־שָׁם where, as (§ 85, D 4)

אֹשֶׁר happiness; *plur. constr* אַשְׁרֵי blessings, salvation

אֵת or אֶת־ 1 sign of the accusative; 2 with, by (Difference of both in combination with suffixes § 74)

אַתָּה thou (pag 44)

אָתוֹן she-ass.

אַתֶּם and אַתֵּן you (pag 44)

אֶתְמוֹל yesterday

ב

בְּ *prep pref* (the lat *in* in all significations) in, at, by, with, near, to

בְּאֵר שֶׁבַע (well of the oath) *propr n* city of Bersabee

בָּדַל *Hi* he divided, separated

בָּהַל *Ni* he was vehemently disturbed, terrified; *Pi.* he hastened

בְּהֵמָה cattle

בּוֹא 1 he entered; 2 he came *Hi* he brought

בָּזָה (id בּוּז) he despised

בָּחַר he chose, selected Hence· *part Ni* eligible, precious, excellent

בָּטַח he confided, he was quiet, secure

בֶּטַח security לָבֶטַח securely

בֵּין *constr stat* of בַּיִן (interval), *prep* between

בִּין he observed, understood

בִּינָה understanding, prudence

בַּיִת 1 house, 2 family (§ 69)

בֵּית־לֶחֶם house of bread, *propr n* Bethlehem

בָּכָה he wept; *fut. apoc.* וַיֵּבְךְּ.

בְּכִי the weeping

בִּלְתִּי 1 *adv* not, 2. *prep* without, 3. *conj* without (that); לְבִלְתִּי so that not (§ 96)

בֵּן (§ 96) 1 son, *plur* children; 2 *trop.* a son of 90 years, that is 90 years old (lat *natus*)

בָּנוֹת *coll* daughters, *see* בַּת.

בָּנָה he built

בִּנְיָמִין son of fortune; *propr n* Benjamin, tribe of Benjamin

בְּעַד *prep* 1. behind, 2 between, 3 at (בְּעַד יָד at the side)

בְּעִיר *coll.* cattle, flocks

בָּעַר he burned, *trans* and *intrans*

בָּקַע he split

בָּקָר *coll* horncattle.

בֹקֶר the morning.

בָּקַשׁ 1 he sought, 2. he endeavored

בָּר corn, wheat

בָּרָא he created, made.

בָּרַח he fled

בְּרִית covenant, alliance; root בָּרָה he cut (ὅρκια τέμνειν).

בָּרַךְ he bent his knees, *Pi* he blessed

בְּרָכָה blessing, happiness; root בָּרַךְ.

בָּשָׂר flesh

בָּשַׂר *Pi* and *Hi* he announced (glad tidings)

בַּת *plur.* בָּנוֹת daughter, girl.

ג.

גְּבוּל terminus, limit, confines, boundaries, circuit.

גִּבּוֹר strong, hero.

גָּדוֹל great, large, tall.

גָּדַל he grew up, he was great

גּוֹי people; *plur* espec is said of other nations than the Israelites, of the gentiles

גָּלָה he revealed; *Ni.* he was open, manifest.

גַּם *adv.* also.

גַּן garden; גָּנַן he fortified.

גַּרְגְּרוֹת neck

גֹּשֶׁן *propr n* Gessen region, land of Goshen

ד

דָּבָר 1. word, 2 thing, 3. something

דָּבַר he sowed, hence, he spoke (sowed word)

דְּבַשׁ honey

דָּגָה *coll.* fish

דֹּב (דוב) bear.

דָּוִד beloved, David; *propr n*

דֶּלֶת door, *dual* דְּלָתַיִם, *constr.* דַּלְתֵי *pr* leaves of door

דָּם blood

דָּן *propr n.* Dan

דַּעַת (*inf.* from יָדַע he knew) knowledge, intelligence, understanding

דֹּר generation, race.

דֶּרֶךְ way.

דָּרַשׁ he sought.

ה

הַ article (§ 51) the.

הֲ *adv* of interrogation (§ 72)

הוּא *f* הִיא *pron III pers* he, she, it (pag. 44)

הוּם he disturbed; *Ni.* he was moved

הוֹרְדוֹס *propr. n.* Herod.

הִיא *see* הוּא.

הָיָה *fut* יִהְיֶה *apoc.* יְהִי (§ 43, not 4) 1. he was, 2 he became, 3 it happened, came to pass, 4 it came out, was ordered.

הֵיטֵב *adv* very well, accurately; *inf Hi. v.* יָטַב he was good

הֵיכָל temple.

הָלְאָה (הָלָא) interval, with ה parag) after this, henceforth

הָלַךְ (§ 39) he went.

הֲלֹם *adv* hither

חָם and חָן *pron III pers plur.*
they (pag. 44)

הָמוֹן 1. noise, 2 multitude; root
הָמָה he made a noise

הֵנָּה *adv.* hither.

הֵן and הִנֵּה *interj.* behold, with
suff. הִנְנִי behold me, הִנּוּ there
he is, הִנֶּנּוּ here we are

הַר mountain.

הָתַל *Pi* הִתֵּל he deceived, illuded

ז

זֹאת *see* זֶה

זָבַח he immolated, sacrificed.

זֶבַח 1 sacrifice, 2 victim.

זֶה *m* זֹאת *f pron demonstr* this,
that.

זָהָב gold

זָהַר *Hi.* he was shining; *Ni* he
was informed, warned

זוּב he flowed; זָבַת *constr. stat.*
fem part Kal

זָכַר he remembered; *Hi* reminded,
made mention   Hence: זֵכֶר or
זֶכֶר memory, name, fame.

זָמַר *Pi* he sang

זָעַק he cried

זָקֵן 1 old man, 2 elder.

זָקָן beard.

זֶרַע 1 seed, 2. race, nation.

ח

חָבַשׁ he bound, saddled, equipped

חֲגוֹר cincture, belt

חִוִּי Hevite, a Canaanite people

חוּס he spared *(prop.* looked with
pity on . .)

חָזוֹן vision, revelation

חָזַק he held, he strengthened, *Hi*
encouraged himself.

חָטָא he sinned. Hence:

חַטָּא sinner.

חַי *adj* alive   In swearing:
חַי יהוה as the Lord lives

חָיָה 1 he lived, 2 he revived.

חַיָּה *constr. st* חַיַּת animal

חָכָם wise, wise man

חָכַם he was wise

חָכְמָה wisdom

חָלָב milk, from חָלַב he was fat.

חֵלֶב fat, the best

חֲלוֹם dream; *inf* of חָלַם he
dreamed.

חָלַל he opened; *Hi* he commenced

חָלַק he was polished, even, *part.*
pass polished

חֲלִיפוֹת שְׂמָלֹת change; חֲלִיפָה
changes of clothes, festal gar-
ments.

חֲמוֹר ass

חָמָס violence; אִישׁ ח' violent

חָמֵשׁ five

חָנָה he encamped

חָנַן *fut* יְחַנַּן and חָן he took pity.

חַנּוּן merciful, gracious

חֲנִית lance.

חִנָּם gratuitously, in vain.

חֶסֶד love, mercy

חָפַז he trembled

חָפְנִי *propr. n* Ophni

חֹק something determined, law,
precept.

חֵק bosom (חיק)

חָקַר he inquired, spied, explored.

חֶרֶב sword.

חֹרֵב *propr n.* Horeb, western
height of Sinai

חָרֵד worried, anxious; root חָרַד.

חָרָה he was incensed, burned

חָרִישׁ the ploughing, time of
ploughing, root

חָרַשׁ *prop* he ploughed; then, he

worked, labored. *figur* he contrived.

חָרַף *Pi.* he vituperated, cursed.

חָשַׂךְ he kept back, refused

חָשַׁךְ *prop* it was dark; *Hi* he obscured Thence:

חשֶׁךְ darkness

חִתִּי Hethite, a Canaanite people

חֹתֵן father in law (*part*)

ט

טָבַע he sank into something.

טוֹב 1 he was good, 2. *adj* good, beautiful

טוּב the good, the best

טָעַן he loaded, burthened

טַף *coll* the progeny, little ones, children

טֶרֶם *adv.* not yet; בְּטֶרֶם before *conj.* (§ 86)

י

יָאַל *Hiph* הוֹאִיל he began, consented

יְבוּסִי Jebusites, inhabitants of Jerusalem.

יָד 1 hand, also power, violence, 2 side; בְּיַד by means of, through

יָדַע 1. he saw, 2 he knew, recognized, 3. experienced; *Pi* he showed; *Hi* he demonstrated, made known, taught; *Hithp* he made himself known.

יְהוּדָה (the praised one) *propr n* Juda, one of the sons of Jacob Tribe of Juda

יְהוּדִים the Jews

יְהוָֹה the name of God (§ 79, 2 b note), the dord.

יְהוֹשֻׁעַ (help of Jehova) *propr n* Josue

יוֹם (§ 69) day; הַיּוֹם often· today (§ 77); יוֹם יוֹם day by day, daily (§ 82, 2)

יַחַד union, connection; *adv* together; with suffixes יַחְדָּו they together

יָחִיד only; root יָחַד

יָטַב 1 he was good, 2. he pleased

יַיִן wine

יָכֹל *fut (Hophal)* יוּכַל he was able, he could

יָלַד he brought forth (peperit) Thence·

יֶלֶד child, boy, youth

יַלְקוּט sack, pocket, bag; root לָקַט

יָסַף he added, continued, increased Hence the *part*

יוֹסֵף *propr n* Joseph

יַעֲקֹב (insidiator) *propr n.* Jacob (also יִשְׂרָאֵל), ancestor of the Israëlites

יָפֶה beautiful

יָצָא he went out, *Hi.* he carried out, brought

יָצַב *Hithp* he placed himself, he stood

יִצְחָק (he laughs) *propr n* Isaac

יָקָר dear, precious; hence: rare

יָרֵא he feared; *Ni.* the same

יָרַד he went down, descended; *Hi.* he brought down

יְרוּשָׁלַיִם *propr n* Jerusalem

יְרִיחוֹ *propr n* Jericho

יִרְמְיָהוּ (Jehova throws) *propr n* Jeremias

יָרַע he was bad, he displeased

יָרַשׁ he took possession of, inherited; *Ni* he was robbed, impoverished

יִשְׂרָאֵל (fighter of God) *propr n* of the kingdom and people of Israël

יֵשׁ there is, it is, is on hand (§ 72, 99)

יָשַׁב he sat, dwelt

יֹשֵׁב inhabitant; *part* of יָשַׁב

יֵשׁוּעַ (contracted from יְהוֹשׁוּעַ) Jesus.

יְשׁוּעָה salvation, felicity

יָשַׁע *Hi* הוֹשִׁיעַ he helped, saved

יָשַׁר he was straight; *Pi* he made straight, even

יָשָׁר *adj* straight, right, just

יֹשֶׁר righteousness, justice

יָתוֹם orphan.

יִתְרוֹ *propr. n* Jethro

כ

כְּ 1 *prep.* like (§ 53), 2 *adv* about, 3 before infinitives: when, as

כָּבֵד, כבד he was heavy; *Hithp* he made himself heavy, weighty, he boasted

כָּבֵד *adj* heavy, weighty

כָּבָה he extinguished

כָּבוֹד prop weight, then, honor, glory

כֹּה *adv* 1 thus, 2. here, there

כֵּהֶה feeble, extinct   Root

כָּהָה he was feeble, he extinguished; *Pi* he rebuked, prohibited

כֹּהֵן priest; *part.* of כָּהַן

כּוֹכָב star

כּוּל he measured; *Pilp* כִּלְכֵּל he supported, fed

כֹּחַ force, power, strength, violence.

כָּחַד *Pi* and *Hi* he hid, concealed

כִּי *conj* 1. that, 2. because, for, 3 but

כִּידוֹן lance

כֹּל or כָּל־ prop universality, whole, hence 1 all, entire, 2 each

כֶּלֶב dog

כָּלָה he was finished, completed; *Pi* he finished

כְּלִי a vase, instrument (§ 69); *plur* furniture

כֵּן *adv* justly, so; לָכֵן therefore

כְּנַעַן *propr n* land of Canaan

כְּנַעֲנִי Canaanite

כִּסֵּא and כְּסֵה chair, throne; root כָּסָה he covered

כְּסִיל a fool, a transgressor, a blasphemer; root כָּסַל he was rude

כֶּסֶף 1 silver, 2 silver-coin, pieces of silver, root כָּסַף he was pale

כָּעַס he was angry, annoyed

כַּעַס anger, indignation.

כַּף *dual* כַּפַּיִם *prop.* something hollow, hand.

כָּפַר he covered; *Hithp* he was expiated

כְּרוּב cherub

כָּרַת he cut off, he rooted out, he destroyed. (He made an alliance)

כָּתַב he wrote

ל

לְ *prep pref* sign of the dative (§ 53, § 80, c d)

לֹא *adv* not

לֵבָב, לֵב heart

לַבָּה flame

לְבוֹנָה incense; root לָבֵן he was white

לְבַד alone

בְּטַח s לָבֶטַח

לָבַשׁ he put on, *Hiph* he clad

לוּחַ tablet.

לָחַם *Ni.* he waged war, he fought

לֶחֶם 1 food, victuals, 2 bread

לָחַץ he oppressed, vexed.

לַחַץ oppression, calamity.

לֵוִי levite

לַיִל night, with ה parag לַיְלָה by night, night

לָמַד he learned, *Pi* he taught

לְמַטָּה down, downwards, below; root נָטָה he extended

לֵץ scoffer (at goodness); *part. of verb* לוּץ

לָקַח (§ 37) 1 he took, he caught, 2 he brought, he fetched

לִקְרַאת *inf v* קָרָא he met, occurred; hence before, in front of

לָשׁוֹן tongue

מ

מִן see מֵ

מֵאָה *plur.* מֵאוֹת hundred

מְאֹד *pr* strength, vehemence, hence: *adv* vehemently, much; עַד־מְאֹד very vehemently, yet more

מְאוּמָה something, contr from מָה וּמָה

מַאֲכֶלֶת a knife; root אָכַל he ate

מָאַן *Pi* he refused, declined

מַגֵּפָה plague, calamity, defeat; root נָגַף he struck, defeated.

מִדְבָּר desert

מַדְוֶה garment.

מַדּוּעַ why?

מִדְיָן *propr. n* Madian.

מָה and מֶה 1 *interrog pron* what? (§ 48), 2 *adv* how? בַּמֶּה (pr. in what?) by what thing? לָמָה why?

מָהַר he hastened

מַהֵר quickly, immediately

מוּסָר castigation, discipline

מוּת he died, *Pi* and *Hi* he killed.

מוֹת *constr st* מוּת death

מִזְבֵּחַ altar; root זָבַח

מָזוֹן victuals, food; root זוּן he nourished

מִחְיָה preservation of life, welfare.

מַחֲנֶה camp; root חָנָה.

מָחַץ *Pi* he broke, struck, repressed

מָחָר tomorrow.

מַחֲשָׁבָה *plur* thought, plot; root חָשַׁב

מִי *interrog pron* who? (§ 48)

מַיִם water (§ 69)

מַכְאוֹב sorrow, affliction; root כָּאַב he was suffering

מַכָּה wound, defeat; root נָכָה he struck

מָכַר he sold; *Ni* he was sold

מַלְאָךְ messenger, angel

מְלוּכָה kingdom, royal power

מִלְחָמָה war; root לָחַם

מָלַךְ he reigned, was king, *Hi.* he caused somebody to reign; he made s king

מֶלֶךְ king

מִן, more used מ or מֶ, *pref* (§ 53), 1. from, 2 out, 3 *comparative* before, more than; *suff* מִמֶּנִּי, מִמֶּנּוּ (§ 74).

מִנְחָה gift, tribute, offering

מָעַד he staggered; מוֹעֲדֵי רָגֶל whose feet are unsteady.

מְעִיל cloak, gown.

מִמַּעַל *adv* over (root עָלָה); from over, above

מַעַן counsel, purpose; hence: לְמַעַן 1 *prep* for, on account of, 2 *conj* in order that

מַעֲרָכָה army, troops

מַפְרֶקֶת neck

מָצָא he found, attained, it happened

מִצְוָה mandate, command

מֵצַח forehead

מִצְרַיִם Egypt and *coll* the Egyptians

מָקוֹם place; root קוּם

מַקֵּל staff, stick; *plur* מַקְלוֹת.

מִקְנֶה possession

מוֹקֵשׁ snare, *metaph* ambush, way-laying, cause of sin; root יָקֵשׁ.

מֹר myrrh; root מָרַר he was bitter

מַרְאֶה and מַרְאָה 1 aspect, 2. appearance, 3 vision; root רָאָה

מֹרִיָּה *propr n* mount Moria

מַרְפֵּא lemency, meekness

מִרְמָה fraud, deceit

מַשְׂכִּיל prudent, kind, pious; root שָׂכַל

מֹשֶׁה *propr n* Moses

מָשִׁיחַ the anointed one, the Messiah; root מָשַׁח

מָשַׁל he commanded, ruled, *Hi* he gave supreme power

מִשְׁפָּט 1 judgment, 2 right, law; root שָׁפַט

מַשָּׁאוֹן fraud, depravity; root נָשָׁא

מַתָּן gift, corruption; root נָתַן.

נ

נָא *partic* of encouragement: do! and of request: I beg, I pray

נָבִיא prophet

נָבַט *Hi* he looked at, he viewed

נָגַד *Hi* he indicated, announced, related

נָגַף he struck, he beat

נָגַשׂ he impelled, he urged, he compelled

נָגַשׁ he touched, approached

נָהַג he led, drove, agitated

נְהִי lamentation

נוּס he fled

נָחַם *Ni* pr he sighed, hence· he was consoled

נְחֹשֶׁת brass, brazen

נָטַשׁ *pr* he crushed, hence: 1 he threw away, omitted, forsook, 2 he spread, scattered

נָכָה *Hi* 1 he struck, threw, upset, defeated, 2 he killed

נָסָה *Pi* he explored, tried, tempted.

נָסַע he moved his camp, departed

נַעַל shoe, sandal

נַעַר 1 boy, youth, 2 servant

(וּת) נְעוּרִים root נַעַר youth, child-hood

נָפַל he fell, *Hi* he let fall

נֶפֶשׁ soul, mind, living thing

נָצַב same as יָצַב he placed; *Ni* he stood

נָצַל *Hi* he took out, rescued, liberated

נָצַר 1 he preserved, saved, 2. he observed, 3 he guarded, 4 he fought against

נָצְרַת *propr n* Nazareth

נֵר lantern, light, lamp; root נ־יר he gave light

נָשָׂא 1 he took up or out, carried out, 2 he carried, bore

נָשִׁים *plur* women; *constr st* נְשֵׁי.

נְשִׁיקָה kiss, flattery; root נָשַׁק

נָשַׁל he put off, doffed

נָשַׁק he kissed

נָתַן (§ 37, note) he gave

ס

סְבָך a thicket; root סָבַך he twisted, entangled

סָגַר he closed, locked; *Pi* he gave over, transmitted, delivered

סוּר 1 he receded, 2 he approached; *Hi.* he removed

סָכָל fool.

סָמַךְ he propped, stayed; *Ni.* he leaned on

סנה bush, thornbush

סָפַר he counted; *Pi* he told, said, narrated

ספר a writer, a scribe

סֵפֶר 1. book, 2 letter

סָתַר he concealed; *Hi* same.

סֵתֶר secret, hidden thing, mystery

ע

עָבַד 1. he worked, 2 he served

עֶבֶד servant, slave

עָבַר he passed, went over; *Hi.* he brought over.

עברי Hebrew

עֲגָלָה chariot

עַד until, to

עֵדֶן *propr n.* Paradise.

עֵדֶר flock, herd

עוֹד 1. again, 2. yet, further

עֹוִין perverse, envious; root עִין

עָוֹן *constr st* עֲוֹן wrong, iniquity; root

עָוָה he was wrong, sinned

עוֹלָם 1. eternity, 2 *adv* for ever; root עָלַם he hid, concealed

עוֹף bird, *coll* fowl

עָזַב he left, abandoned

עַיִן *constr st* עֵין eye.

עִיר city; *plur irreg* עָרִים (§ 69)

עַל *prep* over, up, in, after, around; מֵעַל from over, above

עָלָה he ascended, went up; *Hi* 1) he led up, 2 he offered.

עֹלָה sacrifice, victim

עֵלִי *propr n* Heli

עָלַם he absconded, concealed

עֶלֶם youth (boy)

עַם people; root עָמַם he gathered.

עִם *prep* 1. with, 2 by, near

עָמַד 1 he stood, 2 he remained, 3 he delayed; *Hi* he located, placed

עָמַק he was deep; *Hi.* he made deep

עֵמֶק a valley

עָנָה he answered, began, sang or played.

עֳנִי misery, suffering

עָנָן a cloud

עָפָר dust, soil

עֵץ tree, wood

עֵצָה counsel; root יָעַץ he counseled

עָצַב *Ni* he was saddened

עָקַד he bound, chained

עָרַךְ he put in order, in battle array

עָרֵל uncircumcised, pagan

עָרַץ he feared

עָשָׂה he did, made, acted

עָשׂוֹר *f* עֲשָׂרָה ten (§ 71).

עָשָׁן smoke.

עֵת time

עַתָּה now

פ

פ = פלני 'somebody

פֶּגֶר corpse

פֶּה (§ 69) mouth; *fig* voice, command; כפי according to

פֹּה *adv* here, hither

פּוּג he grew cold; *Ni* he became rigid, torpid

פִּינְחָס *propr n* Phineas.

פְּלֵיטָה help, salvation

פְּלִשְׁתִּים *gent n.* of the Philistines

פֶּן lest, not (lat *ne,* greek μή)

פָּנָה *sing* not used; *plur* פָּנִים face with *prep* לִפְנֵי in face of, before; מִפְנֵי from before; עַל פְּנֵי before, toward, in

פַּעַם *pr* stroke; hence פַּעַם אַחַת once; כְּפַעַם בְּפַעַם now as before.

פְרִזִּי *gent n.* Pherezite, Canaanite people

פְרִי fruit; root פָּרָה he brought forth.

פָרַץ he broke, dispersed; *Ni* he was diffused, spread

פָּשַׁט he put off, doffed

פָּתַח he opened

צ

צֹאן *coll* flock, that is, sheep and goats

צָבָא *plur* צְבָאוֹת armies, hosts

צֵדָה victuals, especial. provision of them, root צוד he hunted.

צַדִּיק just

צֶדֶק justice, right, law

צִוָּה *Pi* he ordered, commanded

צַוָּאר (צַוָּר) neck, *plur* צַוָּארִים, *constr* צַוְּארֵי has significat of *sing*

צָלַל he sounded, tingled

צַלְמָוֶת shadow of death

צִנָּה shield

צָעִיר small, little, contemptible; root צָעַר.

צְעָקָה clamor; root צָעַק

צָפָה he looked on; *Pi* he considered, expected, laid ambushes or snares

ק

קֶדֶם *adv* of place· in front of, before; *subst* East

קָדַשׁ he was holy; *Pi.* he declared holy, sanctified, consecrated.

קָהַל he called (not used); *Hi.* he convoked, congregated.

קָהָל meeting, assembly.,

קוֹבַע helmet

קוֹל voice, sound, fame

קוּם 1 he rose, 2. he stood; *Pi.* קִיֵּם he confirmed; *Hi* he rose, he did, he made rise, excited.

קָטַל he killed

קֵץ end, *verb.* קָצַץ he cut off, broke off

קָלַל he was small; *Pi* he cursed, brought a curse upon himself.

קָלַע *Pi* he shot, he darted

קֶלַע a sling

קָצִיר harvest, season of the harvest,

קָצַף he was inflamed with anger, was angry.

קָרָא I 1 he called, 2. he cried, 3 he named, 4 he recited; II he met (somebody)

קָרַב he acceded, approached, *Hi.* he brought, offered

קֶרֶב inside of a thing, middle

קָרוֹב near; root קָרַב.

קֶרֶן horn

קָרַע he tore, rent, broke asunder.

קָשַׁר he bound, *Pi* same

קֶשֶׁת bow, rainbow; root קוש he extended

ר

רָאָה he saw, experienced; *Ni* he was seen, appeared

ראש 1. head, 2 top, first, prince.

רֵאשִׁית beginning.

רַב *adv* much, enough

רִבּוֹת ten thousand (§ 71)

רָגַז he was disturbed; *Hi.* he provoked, irritated.

רֶגֶל 1. foot, 2 feet

רֹדֵף *part.* persecutor

רוּחַ wind, spirit, soul, mind; *v.* רוּחַ he breathed

רוּעַ and רִיעַ he make a noise, he shouted, he gave cries of joy, of war

רוּץ he ran, hastened; *Hi* he fetched hurriedly

רָחָב wide, spacious; root רָחַב

רָחַם he loved, attended, nursed

רַחוּם merciful; root רָחַם he was charitable.

רָחֵל *propr n.* Rachel

רָחֹק far (*inf* of רָחַק)

רָכַשׁ he acquired

רָמָה *propr. n* Rama, a city.

רַע *f.* רָעָה wicked, bad

רֵעַ friend, companion, neighbor.

רָעָב hunger, famine

רָעָה he fed, tended, ruled

רֵעָה friend

רָשָׁע a bad man, a sinner.

שׂ

שָׂדֶה field

שֶׂה small cattle, sheep

שׂוּם and שִׂים 1. he put, sat, lay, 2. preserved, made

שָׂחַק he laughed; *Pi* he played

שָׂכַל he was prudent; *Hi.* acted prudently

שָׂמַח he rejoiced, was happy; *Pi* and *Hi* he rejoiced (another)

שִׂמְחָה joy.

שִׂמְלָה dress

שָׂנֵא he hated

שַׂר (צָבָא) prince, chief of an army.

שׁ

שָׁאַל he asked; *Ni* he asked for, begged

שְׁאֵרִית remnant

שְׁבִיעִי the seventh.

שָׁבַע he swore; *Ni* same

שִׁבְעָה seven *f* שֶׁבַע (§ 71)

שָׁבַר he broke; *Pi* he crushed

שָׁבַת he ceased, rested; *Hi* he smoothed, placated

שַׁדַּי the Almighty, *epith.* of God (*plur majestat* of שַׁד mighty, powerful, § 79, 2)

שָׁוְא vanity, inanity; *adv* in vain, uselessly; root שׁוא he was bad, angry

שׁוּב he returned; *Hi* he brought back

שׁוֹר ox

שֹׁחַד a present, gift

שָׁחָה he bent; *Hithpael* he bent himself, adored, worshiped (§ 43, note 5)

שָׁחַט he immolated, slaughtered

שַׁחַר dawn

שִׁיר he sang.

שִׁית 1. helaid, 2 made somebody something

שָׁכַב he lay down, slept

שָׁכַח he forgot; *Ni pass.*

שָׁכַם *Hi* he arose early.

שָׁלֹה and שִׁלוּ *propr n* Silo, a city.

שָׁלַח 1 he sent, 2 he sent word, announced, 3 extended, proffered.

שָׁלִישׁ (שָׁלֹשׁ) a musical instrument, an organ, a *sistrum.*

שְׁלִישִׁי the third

שִׁלֵּם retribution, reward

שָׁלַף he extracted, drew.

שָׁלֹשׁ *f* שָׁלֹשָׁה three.

שְׁלֹשִׁים thirty (§ 71).

שִׁלְשׁם third day, day before yesterday

שָׁם *adv of place and time*· there,
then; שָׁמָּה (ה parag) thither

שֵׁם name, fame, good name.

שְׁמֹנֶה *f.* שְׁמֹנָה eight.

שָׁמַיִם heaven

שָׁמַע he heard.

שָׁמַר 1 he watched, guarded, 2 observed, *Hithp* he bewared of

שָׁנָה year; *plur* שָׁנִים; *dual.* שְׁנָתַיִם
two years

שְׁנַיִם *f.* שְׁתַּיִם two (§ 71)

שָׁעַן *Ni* he rested on, he leaned

שַׁעַר door, gate.

שָׁפַט he judged.

שֹׁפֵט judge

שָׁקַד he remained awake, did not
sleep

שִׁרְיוֹן breastplate

שֵׁרֵת *Pi* he ministered, served.

ת

תֵּבֵל (root יָבַל) the globe, the world.

תָּוֶךְ *constr. st* תּוֹךְ middle

תּוֹרָה doctrine, divine law.

תַּחַת *prep* 1 under, 2 for, instead
of; root תוח

תּוֹכֵחָה penalty, punishment, retribution

תַּמְרוּרִים bitterness(es), anguish

תָּעַב *Pi.* he was abominable.

תַּעַר scabbard

תֹּף *plur* תֻּפִּים drum, timbrel

תְּרוּעָה tumult, warcry, great shout;
root רוּץ

תְּשׁוּעָה help, salvation, victory;
root שָׁוַע

תִּשְׁעִים ninety

www.ingramcontent.com/pod-product-compliance
Lightning Source LLC
Chambersburg PA
CBHW060358090426
42734CB00011B/2175